Transparency and Information Asymmetry in Financial Markets

International Banking and Securities Law

Volume published in this Brill Research Perspectives title are listed at *brill.com/rpbs*

Transparency and Information Asymmetry in Financial Markets

A Critical Perspective

By

Daniel Bar Aharon

BRILL

LEIDEN | BOSTON

This paperback book edition is simultaneously published as issue 4.4 of *International Banking and Securities Law*, DOI: 10.1163/24056936-12340012.

Library of Congress Control Number: 2023933039

Brill Open Access options can be found at brill.com/openaccess.

Typeface for the Latin, Greek, and Cyrillic scripts: "Brill". See and download: brill.com/brill-typeface

ISBN 978-90-04-53702-6 (paperback)
ISBN 978-90-04-54907-4 (e-book)

This book is printed on acid-free paper and produced in a sustainable manner.

Contents

Transparency and Information Asymmetry in Financial Markets

A Critical Perspective

Daniel Bar Aharon
Lauder Business School, Vienna, Austria
dbar317@gmail.com

Abstract

The paper deals with the application of aspects of behavioral finance in the context of investor protection reflected in EU financial regulation which puts an emphasis on disclosure requirements. Traditionally, financial regulatory frameworks maintain a status que assumption of "rational investors" contained within neoclassical economic theory, however reoccurring financial incidents have exposed a critical flaw in this understanding, consequently requiring a further examination of behavioral aspects within the context of financial regulation. It remains ambiguous how regulators may best use findings from behavioral finance to address flaws in their investor protection tools. Furthermore, neither expanding disclosure obligations nor enforcing a tougher paternalistic approach may suffice in their intent.

Keywords

financial regulation – investor protection – mandated disclosure regime – information paradigm – behavioral finance – market discipline

1 Introduction

The following paper is an excerpt of the authors master thesis which conducted a critical analysis of the prevailing regulatory tool of disclosure in the context of investor protection and the effective gains in information coherency

 | DOI:10.1163/9789004549074_002

and market discipline. Market discipline refers to market participants rationally managing their risks by making use of publicly disclosed information by financial institutions (World Bank Group, 2019, p. 55). Specifically, this work aims to critically explore the European Union's mounting regularity frameworks pertaining to transparency through mandated disclosure requirements within the purview of traditional investor protection regulation in financial markets.

Financial regulators and scholars view transparency as a fundamental pillar of any securities market (Pattanayak, 2018, p. 1; World Bank Group, 2019, p. 42). However, recurring research conducted on the subject finds that regulation may have reached its peak when it comes to investor protection by means of added disclosure obligations. (Bainbridge 1999, p. 1023; Flannery & Sorescu 1996, p. 1347).

Financial regulation, specifically those which relate to investor protection have particularly been subjected to the EU regulatory spotlight in the devastating aftermath of the Great Financial Crisis (GFC) (Jacques, 2009, p. 4; Goodhart, 2008, p. 331; Ben-Shahar & Schneider, 2010, p. 682; Plato-Shinar & Weber, 2015, p. 233). Financial disclosure has been subjected to stringent and costly regulatory intervention, with contested evidence concerning its effectiveness in enhancing market discipline (Masciandaro & Quintyn 2013, p. 265; Flannery & Sorescu, 1996, p. 1349). While the "regulatory pendulum" is currently heavily swayed towards a stricter supervisory environment (Weiss & Kammel, 2015, p. 4), it brings forth a vigor debate amongst the more liberalized members of the financial markets who must contend with the ebb and flow of shortsighted governance as to the true utility behind these tightening regulatory regimes.

EU financial markets are historically heavily regulated, the standard EU response of amending or adding new regulation in the face of every challenge is a topic of much criticism (Plato-Shinar & Weber, 2015, p. 233; Jacques, 2009, p. 59). There is a continuous discussion in financial circles regarding the topic with rather vague or unconvincing propositions. Unless Regulators find a sustainable and effective structural balance in their mounting regulatory frameworks, the regulatory pendulum will surely continue swinging towards tighter paternalistic norms to the determent of the industry, retail investors and to the robustness of the free markets (Weiss & Kammel, 2015, p. 24; Colaert, 2017, p. 2).

In any case, there is a broad understanding of the need for a stable, efficient and long-lasting regulatory framework that seeks to enhance investor protection while addressing the limitations of information disclosure on market discipline. The foundation of the analysis will rest on the disciplines of economics, financial law and to a large extent the field of behavioral finance which does not only provide useful foundations for the subject matter but also stimulates some critical interdisciplinary thinking in its nexus to financial regulation. By examining the empirical findings collected by the likes of Daniel Kahneman, Richard Thaler and other leaders in the behavioral field, the paper intends to bring to light the inherent challenges regulators face in addressing investor protection and market discipline.

The conflictingly covered phenomenon in which more disclosed information does not necessarily translate into a more informed investor is one of much practical relevance with broad financial and legal implications. The study shall highlight past research which finds that investors ignore or fail to correctly interpret disclosed information, thus unknowingly exposing themselves to financial risks (Deaves, Dine & Horton, 2006, p. 306; Schwarcz, 2008, p. 1119; Kahneman & Tversky, 1979, p. 264; Islam, 2006, p. 121).

1.1 *Structure of the Paper*

The following Parts delve deep into the literature and provide a critical discussion on the key themes that emerged thought the research. Specifically, Part 2 provides a contextual overview of traditional economic and legal theories in order to lay the groundwork for a critical examination of the regulatory rationale as it pertains to investor protection by means of mandated disclosures. Part 3 presents a summary of the key findings from the field of behavioral finance in order to familiarize the reader with the inherited cognitive errors investors exhibit in their decision-making and its consequences on markets and regulatory effectiveness. Part 4 focuses on specific EU's regulatory frameworks as they pertain to informational asymmetries and investor protection with the aim of linking findings from Part 3 and show that even one of the most regulated financial markets in the world still faces numerous challenges in its attempt to implement effective investor protection norms. Part 5 brings together the combined knowledge of prior chapters and examines the viability of alternative and accompaniment forms of investor protection. The aim is to showcase a few, possibly more effective, measures of investor protection solutions. Part 6 shall summarize the key findings and takeaways of the research.

1.1.1 Conceptual Model

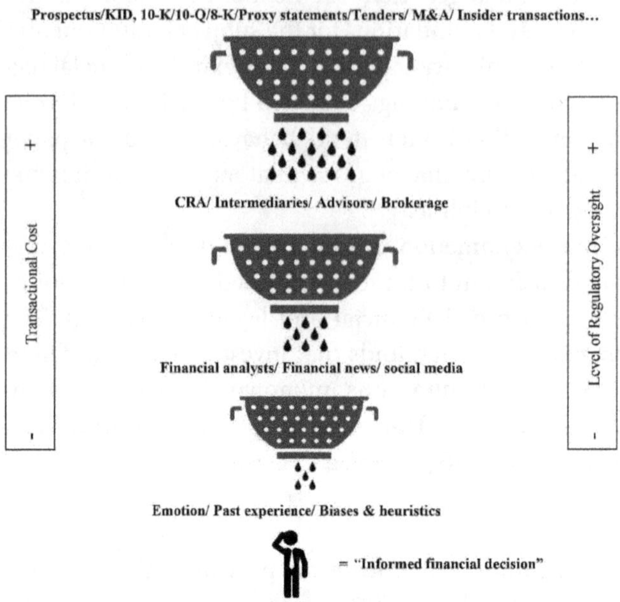

FIGURE 1 "The Colander Effect"
The coined "colander effect" challenges the assumptions of the traditional information paradigm which suggests that increasing the amount of transparent information aids investors in making better informed financial decisions. As publicly disclosed information streams down to the investor, its context gets mediated and reshaped by conflicting interests and the inherently biased interpretations of financial agents (Crockett et al., 2003; Shiller 2000; Andreassen, 1987; Bainbridge, 1999). By the time the "raw information" gets interpreted by the individual it has already gone through multiple levels of biased mediation by which an already inherently biased investor must now base a financial decision upon. A red threat surfaces into the light as transactional costs and regulatory oversight are lowest at the levels closest in informational relevance and comprehension by retail investors.

2 Review of Traditional Economic and Legal Frameworks

The following section shall provide a general overview of traditional economic and legal theories with a critical interpretation as to their assumptions regarding investor protection by means of mandated disclosure. In addition, a critical review of the political rationale of disclosures and regulations will be provided.

2.1 *Neoclassical Economics*

Neoclassical economics is a theory focusing on supply and demand as the driving forces behind the production of goods and services as well as their pricing and consumption; it indicates that investors—together with all other market participants—serve or act as duplicates in line with "homo economicus" assumptions (Herrmann, 1994, p. 41). This theory presumes that all relevant information is accessible and can be equally processed by all participant in order to reach an optimal decision; this rational behavior is commanded by well-defined preferences, which reflect actual costs and benefits (Herrmann, 1994, p. 42). In uncertain situations, people collect all information available to them, evaluate that information and make decisions as per their preferences and choice (Spindler, 2011, p. 317; Camerer, 1995, p. 589). According to the traditional information paradigm, increasing the availability to information ensures fuller transparency and assists investors in making informed investment decisions (Camerer et al., 2003, 1211; Colaert, 2017, p. 3). Disclosure has increasingly been a topic of discussion for many years, but limited conclusions have been made on the conditions in which "effective information" must follow, at least not in so much from the investor's perspective (Masciandaro & Quintyn 2013, p. 265; Flannery & Sorescu, 1996, p. 1349).

Neoclassical theory does not distinguish between quality, length or level of comprehension of information; if investors fulfilled their utopian concept of "homo economicus", then they would be experts in all areas of life, e.g., financial matters or even home repairs (Oehler & Wendt, 2017, p. 182). Although it's common knowledge that investors do not and will not meet this ideal criterion of being fully informed and rational decision-makers, the crux of the issue however lies in the fact that around two-thirds of all investor-protection regulation is based on the assumptions of that exact ideal. (Micklitz, 2014, p. 339; Oehler & Wendt, 2017, p. 180).

2.2 *New Institutional Economics*

The new institutional economics (NIE) provides a framework that takes into account possible informational asymmetry or disadvantage of investors in comparison to the information providers, such as fund managers and financial advisors; in acknowledgment of this disadvantage between principle and agent, NIE permits asymmetries in power for designing and enforcing laws by which contractual parties are financially bound (Weiss & Kammel, 2015 p. 42; Oehler & Wendt, 2017, p. 182).

The primary premise behind NIE is that in the division of labor, an individual should not need to have complete information of everything involved in a given process; asymmetries should thus be viewed as an integral and unavoidable part of our economic systems (Micklitz, 2014, p. 340). Expecting or making investors grip with an overflow of information is in contradiction to these ideas; such expectation would entail investors to have knowledge regarding all their informational needs and possess the capacity to recognize and comprehend all the relevant parts of such information (Oehler & Wendt, 2017, p. 182). However, investors will only know what they want to learn if they have a clear idea of what they need to know—something that is hardly achievable for the majority of financial decisions made in the real world (Oehler & Wendt, 2017, p. 182).

NIE framework indicates that to minimize their disadvantage investors will require simplified information and/or assistance in understanding it; moreover, through legal encouragement, the weak party of the market (the investors) can impose greater competition in the market by demanding higher quality information, especially from financial service providers (Oehler & Wendt, 2017, p. 182). However, a problem arises as most financial products are credence goods, meaning that full information about them is unavailable before and after the contract; therefore, it's impossible to provide complete information ex-ante to investors just on the basis of available forecasts which are already based on weakly correlated statistical measures of past performance (Oehler & Wendt, 2017, p. 182).

2.3 *Self-Correcting Market Mechanisms*

It can be said in defense of the rational behavior assumptions that if market participants behave or act irrationally, in the long run, they will be eliminated by the market mechanism since irrational strategies are bound to be ineffective and unsustainable (Spindler, 2011, p. 318). Thus, the market mechanism of long-run learning effects needs to be considered as they will eliminate irrational and deviating behavior from the market as "learned" market participants would be more skillful and profitable than the others (Camerer, 1995, p. 675; Stiglitz, 1975, p. 284). Particularly, it is in the best interest of financial institutions to behave in rational ways to keep the markets working efficiently (Spindler, 2011, p. 318).

In practice, within the context of informational asymmetries, it is more likely that market participants will envision new tools to fix any transitionary asymmetries, especially by inventing and introducing quality-signaling mechanisms (Spence, 1976, p. 592). The most prominent mechanism involves ratings given to companies or their financial products for signaling to the market and the investors that those particular products are reliable and of better quality than others (Spence, 1976, p. 592). This is the rationale of rating agencies and other financial intermediaries such as advisory or research, who evaluate products and give ratings or recommendations based on their expertise (Spindler, 2011, p. 318; Liu & Thakor, 1984, p. 345). Furthermore, these reputation mechanisms serve to incentivize financial suppliers to make maximum efforts in delivering quality products and services in order to attract secondary market participants who rely on signaling mechanisms to overcome their informational disadvantage in assessing complex financial products (Spindler, 2011, p. 318). Nevertheless, as shall be discussed in the following chapters, the recent past has demonstrated that many of our previous assumptions and theories dealing with the information paradigms, market efficiency, and market mechanisms may turn out to be flawed and invalidated.

2.4 *Traditional Efficiency Model*

The NIE and neoclassical economics theories formulate normative principles that can be used for empirical testing and ultimately for regulatory justification (Salzberger, 2008, p. 24; Spindler, 2011, p. 326). They provide a framework for empirical verification, by prescribing "a blueprint of an ideal efficient market economy, which enables one to identify any pitfalls or gaps of market mechanisms that should be fixed by legal intervention" (Salzberger, 2008, p. 24).

Notably, the traditional efficiency model can identify the "first-best", "second-best", ext. resolution for a given problem which enables legislators to use efficiency criteria during their legal deliberations (Posner, 2007, p. 530). Many legal terms, such as common usage, good faith, etc., which call for a "judgmental interpretation", are not clearly defined by law itself and have an extensive scope of subjectivity in economic analysis (Posner, 2007, p. 530; Spindler, 2011, p. 326). Given the subjective scope of interpretations and the fact that the normative principles are based on false rational assumptions, one could begin to see the infringing challenges in producing effective regulation.

2.4.1 Transparency and Disclosure

2.4.1.1 *Ideal Transparency Conditions*

Transparency, in terms of accessibility to information, is a vital component from the perceptive of all market participants, including regulators, financial intermediaries and retail investors (Oehler & Wendt, 2017, p. 184). While it is not necessarily expected that market participants will make use of every available piece of information, the unavailability of said information might cause investors to miss on an important aspect in decision making as they won't know which information is missing, hidden (Jin, Luca, & Martin, 2015, p. 306). Information access is a basic stipulation for both traditional economic frameworks, but it can only be deemed as a prerequisite if we assume that consumers are rationally bounded (Oehler & Wendt, 2017, p. 184).

Bounded rationality assumes that interpretation of the same piece of information by different individuals is done in uniquely diverse ways (Simon, 1995, p. 15). To minimize likely misinterpretation, the information needs to be "comprehensible", meaning that it must be offered in plain language avoiding the use of technical terms; comprehensibility should reflect that the individuals without expert knowledge can easily understand the information presented to them (Oehler & Wendt, 2017, p. 185).

Information leading towards a financial decision must always be accompanied with alternatives to choose between; even seating on your hands could be such an option (Oehler & Wendt, 2017, p. 186). In a financial context, decisions are viewed as complex due to the vast assortment of possible products and the uncertainty regarding their future performance; making an informed decision is compromised if information on alternative decisions or products are unavailable or lacks comparability (Oehler & Wendt, 2017, p. 186). Therefore, information about the financial products should be put out in a way that they could be compared with similar products; the presentation of comparable information categories, such as associated risk factors, should be standardized across all financial products being offered to retail investors (Oehler & Wendt, 2017, p. 186).

2.4.1.2 *Mandated Disclosure*

Mandated disclosures are amongst the most used techniques for guarding personal autonomy in our modern world (Ben-Shahar & Schneider 2011, p. 649). It is a widely used regulatory tool that aims at improving the quality of people's financial decisions; it particularly aims at protecting the naïve from the sophisticated (Ben-Shahar & Schneider 2011, p. 649). This method mandates the "discloser" (company) to provide the investor or potential investor with all relevant information that they may use for making better decisions; as such, mandating disclosures aims at mitigating companies from abusing their superior position (Ben-Shahar & Schneider, 2011, p. 650). As a tool, mandated disclosures aim to address a real informational concern in our everchanging modern lives, where investors are burdened with an overflow of complex decisions about which they usually have very little experience over.

The themes raised and discussed throughout this paper, are less concerned with the quantity or specificality of information, but rather aims to explore the utility of these disclosures in and of itself. The underlining question is if mandated disclosure, as a regulatory tool, effectively enriches the decision process investors make? Unfortunately, the regulatory tool of disclosure relies on a number of questionable assumptions and its effectiveness requires an unlikely series of aligned interests and collaboration between legislators, disclosers, and investors (Ben-Shahar & Schneider, 2011, p. 651; Weiss & Kammel, 2015 p. 28).

Although mandated disclosure tries to address a serious market concern, it often falls short in achieving its purpose; even where it looks to be succeeding, its costs—in terms of money, utility, and time—largely overshadow its benefits (Ben-Shahar & Schneider, 2011, p. 651). The empirical evidence shows that this regulatory tool often fails in practice, more importantly, its failure is inevitable (Bardach & Kagan, 1982, p. 189).

2.4.2 Critical Review of Disclosures Political and Legal Rational

The public demand for action deluge lawmakers. Many of these demands are inspired by "trouble stories"—independent, though widely publicized events illustrate the apparent short-termism mindset rampant in the political sphere (Ben-Shahar & Schneider, 2011, p. 679). Political pressure, public indignation, and a "sense of duty" incentivize legislators to take on a "sprinkler system" approach as the fear of not doing enough outweigh the rationale of doing what is appropriate (Weiss & Kammel, 2015 p. 19). Particularly, as shown by Bardach and Kagan (1982), "trouble stories" are usually the key catalysts for new regulation; lawmakers in our media-driven world turn individual acts of misconduct or misfortune into wide social problems requiring broader intervention from their part (p. 190). Bureaucratic drive towards more regulation is partly a result of current policy failure, and partly due to new novel risks that might not be systemic threats; however, publicized scandals that expose laxity, corruption, or even stories that expose incompetency in regulatory institutions, spark that growth (Ben-Shahar & Schneider, 2011, p. 690). Goodhart (2007) says it best: "since politicians do not want it to be their own heads that become parted from their bodies, they feel the need to be seen to be taking actions to make sure that that particular disaster never happens again" (p. 62).

A theme that has repetitively been analyzed in this paper questions if mandated disclosure is the best form of regulation for investor protection. Disclosure sounds appealing as it resonates with the fundamental capitalist ideals of free markets and individual autonomy, in addition to its direct association with the accepted rationale of "caveat emptor". However, this "soft law" type of protection is weak as it only requires the provision of discourser but does not supervise over any of the substantive matters in the discourse itself, i.e., risk, costs or quality (Weiss & Kammel, 2015, p. 42). Essentially this means that rather than outright restricting certain products, such as those that are exploitative in their costs, we are given disclosure shopping lists with associated risks and confusing cost estimations. Rather than supervising over the content, regulators prefer to simply mandate all information for which they leave it up to the investor to choose how to make the best use of in their decision process (Ripken, 2006, p. 145). In addition, the autonomy principle supposes that investors themselves can make better decisions than anyone else doing so on their behalf and that people are entitled to have freedom in making their own decisions (Ben-Shahar & Schneider 2011, p. 680).

Lawmakers are attracted to mandated disclosure for several other reasons: 1) Mandated disclosure is the cheaper and more respected approach (Weiss & Kammel, 2015, p. 223). It seems to cost nothing to the government while the brunt appears to be borne by the "villain" in the story, the stronger party (company) that up until now has "supposedly" withheld critical information. 2) It looks easy, mandated disclosure just requires more information to be communicated between parties that are already transacting; in hindsight, it always appears that information that could have led to better decisions and prevented a "trouble-story" should have been present (Ben-Shahar & Schneider 2011, p. 682). 3) It seems obvious, detailed information usually appears relevant during complex decision processes involving future uncertainties; even indifferent market participants would likely say that although disclosers may not be helpful, they can't hurt (Ben-Shahar & Schneider 2011, p. 682).

As such, the rationale of disclosers seems unrefuted; a disclosures failure only leads to the assumption that it should be further enhanced. For instance, despite the ever-growing length and costly compliance of mortgage disclosures, the 2008 subprime mortgage bubble was brewing into a global financial crisis (GFC), largely due in part to the unhinged and risky loaning practices taking place at the time (Schwarcz, 2008, p. 1119). Despite rational suggestions to substantively regulate mortgage practices and enhance supervising over lenders, lawmakers continue to deem disclosures essential in all proposals of regulatory reform (Bar-Gill, 2008, p. 1073).

Legislators' attraction towards mandated disclosure and the "more-is-better mantra" far too often leads them to establish new frameworks or amendments of existing requirements; however, this rational is intrinsically dilutive; only a broadly scoped disclosure can sufficiently accommodate the variety of all possible of circumstances (Ben-Shahar & Schneider 2011, p. 684). Therefore, the scope and length of mandated disclosures seem to only keep mounting up with hardly any pressure of trimming off redundant fat; since it's hard to anticipate what information will be relevant, safety appears to lie in large numbers. Legislators appear to be under an unending pressure to cover newly observed contingencies; this eventually brings about an unintended overload problem, wherein the investors will fail to comprehend, evaluate, or assimilate the information overflow and, in most cases, won't even bother to make use of it (Camerer et al., 1989, p. 1232).

When discussing investor protection, we must also attune ourselves to the paradox of over-protection. The two somewhat inconsistent objectives in investor protection make it difficult to understand what investor protection stands for. On the one hand, should regulations enable autonomy for investors to make any financial decision? Or on the other hand, should enhanced regulation be implemented to protect investors from losses taken on uncalculated risks or obvious mistakes? Unfortunately, as Wiess & Kammel (2015) point out that when an incident occurs, regulators pressured by shortsighted politicians tend to favor over-regulating the markets; the paradox here is that while there might be public and political support for such measures due to fear and uncertainty, the public is not always fully aware of the practicality and long-term consequences of such new measures (p. 16).

Legislators don't appear to have a sustainable solution to the aforementioned issues discussed in this chapter. Unfortunately, when dealing with regulations there's rarely a holy grail solution (Masciandaro & Quintyn, 2014, p. 306). Incomplete disclosure keeps people in the dark, but too much disclosure results in counterproductive overload problems. A seasoned lawmaker could understand that "less is more", but still, they may fear that "less is not enough" (Ben-Shahar & Schneider 2011, p. 688). Critically, it is legislator's incentives (getting paid to make laws) that drive them toward recommending the "easy" path of additional disclosure requirements (Ben-Shahar & Schneider 2011, p. 688). When legislators are overwhelmed with pleas for reform, demanding more disclosure always looks like the obvious solution as its opponents are rare; it showcases real action taken by the lawmakers, all the while, the disclosers (who are most economically burdened) rarely fight back as they prefer disclosure to harsher more restrictive measures (Ben-Shahar & Schneider 2011, p. 684). Simpler alternatives to disclosure are scarce, the dogmatic value of disclosure seems to allude to its political utility rather than towards its intended purpose.

2.4.3 Implicit Costs of Mandated Disclosure

Irrespective of the perceived benefits of the mandated disclosures, does its costs justify or outweigh its benefits? Measuring together the costs and the benefits is just as challenging, while the known costs of mandated disclosure itself are considerable (Hoskins & Labonte, 2015, p. 2). Let's begin by considering a few direct compliance costs and then some implicit costs that are mostly unintended and unrecognized. The mandated disclosure's implementation costs: For instance, disclosers (companies) spend considerable resources to find out what disclosures are required and how to best implement them; this is corroborated by the growing demand for banking compliance jobs that now outnumber research departments (Hoskins & Labonte, 2015, p. 2). As a result, issuers of securities and other financial services must constantly retain specialized legal counsel. Moreover, the costs of acquiring and providing information for disclosers are particularly huge when information is not already collected and assembled; every new requirement involves fixed incremental costs concerning research, drafting work, and dissemination, all of which need additional personnel and training (Hoskins & Labonte, 2015, p. 3).

The high fixed cost incurred with every new mandated iteration has unintended anticompetitive effects. These fixed costs—relating to the information collection, drafting and training of employees—are almost the same for all disclosers irrespective of their size. This gives the bigger institutions an advantage because their per "unit" burden of disclosure is smaller (Easterbrook & Fischel, 1984, p. 689). This ultimately hurts small players trying to enter the market and compete on a level playing field.

Mandated disclosure also has the unintended effects of undermining investors' "self-guard"; disclosure documents provide a "veneer of legality" in financial exchanges, causing buyers to lower their guard (Willis, 2006, 741). The presence of official-looking papers gives the false impression that regulators are on the watch and supervising over the document's specific terms when in fact regulators view these documents more in line as a "caveat imperator"; as such, investors are less suspicious and cautious when taking on positions they might know little about (Willis, 2006, 741). Lastly, mandated disclosures have been shown to exuberate inequity: "It helps most those who need it the least and helps least those who need it the most" (Mandell, 1973, p. 26). Financial disclosures are more helpful to those who are already well-educated and financially well-off; they have the sophistication and resources to find, interpret and assimilate the information (Mandell, 1973, p. 26). As Mandell's (1973) study reveals, knowledge of credit markets by consumers was closely related to education and family income (p. 26).

2.4.4 Outlook

Post-GFC, EU regulators placed the fault of the crisis on disclosure asymmetries with the regulatory assumption that the market cannot be left to its own fruitions. EU financial regulation was built on the precepts of efficient market theories, according to which informational asymmetry can be reduced through disclosures, thus reducing or even eliminating frictions in the market. The overflow of EU disclosure frameworks introduced in the past decade and still being introduced today only confirm these assumptions. Now we could come together and agree that some of these frameworks are not working and need tweaking, thus again giving momentum to the inevitable pendulum swings in regulatory cycles, all of which come at the detrimental cost to the industry and the individual investor.

While there is skepticism about the utility of mandated disclosure, this paper does not contend that it is redundant. Possibly the issue lies in the bureaucratic dynamic and regulatory assumptions—their wish to solve too many problems by over informing everyday decision-makers while expecting them to make thoughtful and informed decisions. The validity of these assumptions will be thoroughly investigated in the next chapter by examining behavioral aspects of decision-makers and the inherent challenge these behaviors pose on regulation.

3 Behavioral Finance: Market and Regulatory Implications

According to established economic theories, firms and individuals' function in fully rational ways, and their only objective is the optimization of their profit; contrastingly, according to behavioral economist Herbert Simon (1955) when a choice with uncertain outcome is to be made, people tend to stray away from behavior that is "strictly rational" (p. 99). Investors, like every other individual, are helpless captives of human behavior (Simon, 1955, p. 100). As Benjamin Graham (1965) said, "we are our own worst enemies" (p. 8). While investors are presumed to be rational by conventional theories, behavioral finance assumes that they are not (Bernstein, 2007, p. 145; Bodie, 2009, p. 418). When considering the fields with the potential to redefine our comprehension of the functioning of financial markets, the behavioral finance discipline cannot be overlooked. It is far from clear how the widely accepted assumptions of the efficient market hypothesis may endure in light of the behavioral sciences (Bodie, 2009, p. 368).

The field of behavioral finance has countlessly demonstrated the inherent limitations of people's cognitive capabilities when it comes to processing information and making even simple financial decisions; often an individual's decision is irrationally influenced by their behavioral or emotional biases/heuristics (Kahneman & Tversky 1979, p. 264; Selten, 1990, p. 649; Baron, 2000, p. 146; Simon, 1955, p. 99). The events leading up to the GFC and its cumulative destructive aftermath may serve as a harsh reminder of our collective irrationality. Perhaps it is time legislators began reconsidering the feeble notions of neoclassical economic theory and the traditional assumptions of "rational agents". The GFC has revealed that even financial professionals suffer from the same irrational cognitive effects which in part provoked the contagion snowball effect seen during the crisis (Hirshleifer, 2011, p. 1533). As such, the discipline of behavioral finance may provide valuable insight for EU legislators in their search towards a regulatory holy grail of investor protection norms. The following chapter shall generalize some prevalent empirical findings from the field of behavioral finance and attempt to contextualize how behavioral errors applied to financial markets could cause regulatory ambiguity in fostering effective investor protection norms.

3.1 *Processing Errors*

3.1.1 Information Overload

Amongst the plethora of processing errors investors make, the effects of information overload could be argued to be amongst the most relevant to this analysis. The objective of disclosure to convey critical information more efficiently to investors is understandable, however, in practice the average investor will not methodically filter through great amounts of pages, nor will they equally possess the ability to distinguish between the quality of information that is provided to them (Spindler, 2011, p. 322). Stemming from Simon's (1955) theory on bounded rationality, information overload or the "curse of knowledge" as Camerer et al. (1989) call it is a cognitive constraint where investors become overwhelmed and discouraged by the amount and/or the complexity of disclosed information, thus opting to ignore some or all of it due to its high transaction cost (p. 1232).

Transaction costs can be differentiated by internal or external costs (Stigler 1961, p. 213; Smith et al., 1999, p. 285). External costs relate to quantifiable financial costs of obtaining the information, whereas internal costs reflect the individuals' cognitive strain in searching, filtering and comprehending the information (Smith et al., 1999, p. 285; Hauser 1993, p. 452). Caplan (2007) explains this phenomenon by graphing the "demand for irrationality" to demonstrate that individuals are more prone to act irrationally with the decrease in the cost of doing so (p. 2). In other words, the consequence of offering a broader and more complex information supply may lead to a steady increase of internal transaction costs trailed by an incline in the demand curve for irrationality (Caplan, 2007, p. 2; Spindler, 2011, p. 322).

Nemours experiments conducted on the subject indicate a negative correlation between the quantity and complexity of information to the likelihood that an investor would opt to read it due to its hefty transaction costs (Ben-Shahar & Schneider 2010, p. 672; Deaves, Dine & Horton, 2006, p. 306). To offset the negative effects of information overload investors often seek professional financial advice and consultation as well as relying on condensed and filtered information provided by rating agencies or financial intermediaries; however, as shall be discussed later in this paper, experts have shown to be equally prone to the some of the same irrational behaviors typically exhibited by retail investors (Spindler, 2011, p. 324).

While accommodative in their motives to protect investors through enforcing additional disclosed information, in practice regulators fail to address the crux of the issue by which investors have been shown to repeatedly fail in making rational investment decisions based on information provided to them (Simon, 1955, p. 100; Posner, 1998, p. 1552; Tversky & Kahneman, 1986, p. 251). "Information is beneficial only to the extent that it can be understood and utilized by the individual to whom it is directed—Evidence suggests that when people are given too much information in a limited time, the information overload can result in confusion, cognitive strain, and poorer decision-making" (Ripken, 2006, p. 160). The principal argument here is that seeing the "source code" is not that same as understanding it (Ananny & Crawford, 2018, p. 6).

The most prominent example of this phenomenon can be seen in almost any end-user license agreement where consumers hastily scroll through or skim the legal fine prints when proceeding in making a purchase (Ben-Shahar & Schneider 2010, p. 671).

Internal transaction costs due to information length and/or complexity are a clear consequence of information asymmetries caused by cognitive constraints. Likewise, the effects of information overload are related to "choice overload" when being offered a large array of complex finical products to choose from (Dhar, 1997, p. 215; de Meza et al., 2008, p. 39). Consequently, it is common for intermediaries to hide some or artificially simplify the complexity and/or the range of potential financial products to avoid purchase hesitancy due to choice overload (Spindler, 2011, p. 323).

3.1.2 Base Rate Neglect

In their journal article titled "On the Psychology of Prediction," Kahneman and Tversky (1973) denote that people give excessive importance to recent experience over their previous beliefs (base rate) when they make estimates and such forecasts are typically very extreme, due to the innate uncertainty of the information they possess (p. 237). This relates to the empirical findings of DeBondt and Thaler (1990) in their journal article titled "Do Security Analysts Overreact?" They argue that the P/E effect (a market anomaly where stocks with low price-to-earnings ratio's often achieve higher returns) is possible to explain via extreme earnings expectations (p. 52). From this perspective, when the predictions of the future earnings of a firm are high, maybe because of positive performance in the recent past, they are typically too high relative to the firm's objective prospects; this causes a high initial P/E, with the subsequent performance being poor when the error is finally recognized by the broader market (DeBondt & Thaler, 1990, p. 56). Ironically, with all their glamor, investing in high P/E firms tend to be the suboptimal choice over the long run (DeBondt & Thaler, 1990, p. 56; Bodie, 2009, p. 390).

Chopra, Lakonishok, and Ritter (1992) similarly found that typically, people don't take into account a sample's size, and merely assume that a small sample functions as the representative of a larger population (p. 240). Thus, they may infer a pattern promptly based on a small sample and conclude excessive trends into the future (Chopra et al., 1992, p. 262). Thus, such patterns can result in overreaction and correction anomalies; when good earnings reports or high stock returns have a short-lived rally, such investors will alter their evaluations about likely future performance, and therefore, create purchase pressure further exaggerating the rally in price (Bodie, 2009, p. 391). Ultimately, the disconnect between price and intrinsic value becomes obvious and the initial error is corrected by the market; remarkably, stocks demonstrating optimal performance in the recent past suffer major reversals around their earnings announcements, thus, indicates that the correction unfolds when investors understand that their initial forecasts were too extreme (Bodie, 2009, p. 391).

3.2 *Behavioral Biases*

Notwithstanding a world with perfect information processing skills, several studies have concluded that people typically tend to make decisions that are not entirely rational with that information (Bodie, 2009, p. 391). The following subchapter will discuss how intrinsic behavioral biases impact how investors inaccurately frame decisions of risk versus return decisions.

3.2.1 Overconfidence

One more phenomenon that one can observe from the financial crisis was increased self-confidence; concerning risk assessment, bank managers and financial intermediaries seemed overconfident about their judgments while not completely understanding the design of the financial products that were trading or selling to their clients (Barber & Odean, 2001, p. 261). People typically overestimate how precise their beliefs or forecasts, while overestimating their abilities (Bodie, 2009, p. 390); consider the tendency of active mutual funds to overestimate their abilities while generally achieving disappointing performance compared to their benchmarks (Bernstein, 2002, p. 222). The same folly is prevalent in retail clients when trying to pick mutual funds based on their past performance (Bernstein, 2002, p. 222). Picking mutual funds can be a highly seductive venture; regrettably, management luck is hardly ever considered when choosing those funds that have recently outperformed (Bernstein, 2002, p. 180). Taking into consideration taxation, this seductive venture can be particularly devastating if the "ponies are switched" too often, as the short-term capital gains will cut deep into account returns (Bernstein, 2002, p. 180).

One example of overconfidence that is worth noting is offered by Barber and Odean (2001), they equated trading activity and returns between men and women; it was found that men (specifically single men) tend to trade very actively when compared to women, which aligns with the literature in psychology regarding greater overconfidence among men (p. 262). They found that frequent trading activity is significantly predictive of poor returns; the top 20% of portfolios ranked by turnover rate demonstrated average returns that are 7% lower when compared to the 20% of the accounts that had the lowest turnover rates (Barber & Odean, 2001, p. 275). They concluded that "trading, and by implication, overconfidence is hazardous to your wealth" (Barber & Odean, 2001, p. 289).

3.2.2 Prospect Theory and Endowment Effect

How do people decide between alternatives that involve risk and uncertainty? Kahneman & Tversky (1979) behavioral experimentations led them to coin the prospect theory in which they claimed that an individual's utility or "emotional weighting" towards a loss is about twice greater to that of a gain; they named this phenomenon of "loss aversion" the endowment effect (p. 263). Put in another way, it is in people's tendency to demand a premium when selling something they already own then they would be willing to spend in purchasing that same thing (Kahneman, Knetsch & Thaler 1991, p. 93).

The implications of the endowment effect have thoroughly been studied in investment decisions of retirement funds; the studies found that investors tend to hold on to losing positions even when selling them at a realized loss would be a wise choice from a wholly objective perspective (Madrian & Shea, 2001, p. 1149; Choi et al., 2002, p. 67). As seen the endowment effect is prevalent after an initial investment decision is made, the above-mentioned studies observed the effect is in play in asset management decisions throughout investors holding time horizons (Spindler, 2011, p. 323). These effects closely resemble Samuelson and Zeckhauser's (1988) research on status quo bias, where investors have been shown to exhibit reluctance in making portfolio changes as any change from their established "baseline portfolio" is perceived as a loss (p. 7).

3.2.3 Framing and Mental Accounting

The way in which our choices are framed to us seem to have an effect on our decisions; for instance, a person might decide to decline a bet if presented with the risk encompassing potential gains, while the same bet may be accepted if described with respect to the risk encompassing possible losses (Tversky & Daniel Kahneman, 1986, p. 252). The framing of a risky venture is usually entirely arbitrary; imagine a coin toss that has a payoff of $50 if it were to fall on tails, now, think of a gift of $50 that comes in tandem with a bet risking a loss of $50 in case the coin toss comes up heads—both cases would result in no gains for heads and $50 for tails (Bodie, 2009, p. 391). However, in the former case, the coin toss is framed as offering a risky gain and the latter involves a framing of risky losses; the variation of such framing could result in varying attitudes toward the bet or investment choice (Statman, 2019, p. 26; Bodie, 2009, p. 392).

A specific form of framing is mental accounting, wherein certain decisions are segregated into categories (Thaler, 1985, p. 200). For instance, a lot of risk may be undertaken by an investor with one investment account, while another account may undertake a conservative position as it is dedicated to

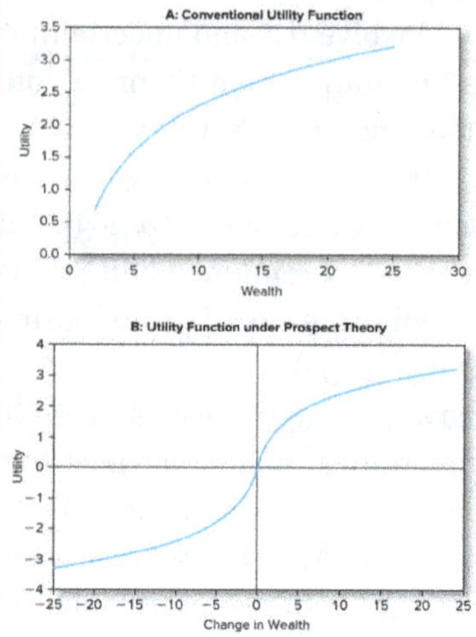

FIGURE 2 Prospect theory utility function. Panel A, illustrates the conventional description of a risk-averse investor. Higher wealth provides higher satisfaction, or "utility," but at a diminishing rate. Panel B, shows a competing description of preferences characterized by "loss aversion." Utility depends not on the level of wealth, as in panel A, but on changes in wealth from current levels. The convex curvature to the left of the origin in panel B will induce investors to be risk-seeking rather than risk-averse when it comes to losses.
BODIE, 2009, P. 393

the education of a child; logically, it may be better to perceive both accounts as a part of the overall portfolio of the investor, wherein the risk-return profiles of each are bundled up to create a unified profile (Statmanm, 2008, p. 79). Mental accounting effects further assist with explaining stock prices momentum; the house money effect is essentially the greater willingness of gamblers to accept new bets in cases where they are currently seating on profits (Bodie, 2009, p. 393). The bet is framed as one that is made using "house money" which is basically with the casino's money and not their own, which is why they are willing to take on higher degrees of risk (Bodie, 2009, p. 393).

3.2.4 Hindsight

One crucial facet of knowledge involves learning from prior experience; when we learn about how something turned out, we attempt to comprehend what resulted in its occurrence and we assess how effectively we or others planned for it (Fischoff, 1982, p. 427). The psychologist Baruch Fischhoff (1982), was first to note that "In hindsight, people consistently exaggerate what could have been anticipated in foresight. People believe that others should have been able to anticipate events much better than they actually did. They even misremember their own predictions so as to exaggerate in hindsight what they knew in foresight" (p. 428).

3.2.5 Availability

Availability shortcuts are used by us while assessing the probability of events based on readily available information within our minds (Statman, 2019, p. 40). Mutual funds that have high returns attract investors merely if these funds' stocks were recently featured in the media; however, availability through the media in no way helps investors garner better returns (Oehler et al., 2018, p. 3) In fact, availability errors increase an investors' tendency to move towards mutual funds that were recently featured holding stocks with high past returns (Oehler et al., 2018, p. 3). Mutual fund managers tend to leverage availability errors as they buy such stocks around the time when the funds' contents are reported, which is a strategy known as "window dressing," and this is usually prevalent among mutual funds that are poorly performing (Solomon, Soltes & Sosyura, 2014, p. 53).

The transactions costs of obtaining accounting information have never been lower, we have an abundance of free online articles and automated push notifications of current earnings announcements (Statman, 2019, p. 41). However, it has been shown that amateur investors don't incorporate "earnings information into their trading, instead, they trade in response to recent stock returns that are vivid but offer no value-relevant information" (Blankespoor et al., 2019, p. 54). It would seem likely that investors who were better informed would garner higher returns; counterintuitively, experiments conducted by Harvard psychologist Professor Paul Andreassen (1990) demonstrated how news junkies who follow frequent news updates on their positions achieve half the returns than those who ignore the news (p. 153). This appears to fall in line with similar claims stemming from the likes of Thaler, Tversky, Kahneman and Schwartz (1997) who wrote in the *Quarterly Journal of Economics* that "Investors with the most data do the worst in terms of money earned" (p. 659).

3.2.6 Disposition Effect

Shefrin and Statman (1985) highlight regret aversion and pride seeking as primary factors in the "disposition effect" (p. 777). In a taxable account, a rational utilitarian maximizing investor would be quick in realizing losses and slow to realize gains, since realized losses lessen one's tax burden while realizing gains early add to them (Shefrin & Statman, 1985, p. 778). However, studies show that the average investor is too quick to realize gains (keen to feel pride) while they are slow to realize losses (fretful to regret), which displays a disposition to "sell winners too early and ride losers too long" (Shefrin & Statman, 1985, p. 778).

A neurological experiment using magnetic resonance imaging (MRI) demonstrated active regret signals in the neural area typically associated with reward processing when a positive return was seen in a stock in which the participant chooses not to buy; in such cases, participants were reluctant to repurchase stocks if their prices rose recently, although repurchasing would have been the optimum choice according to the experiment's design (Frydman & Camerer, 2016, p. 5). Those demonstrating high rates of repurchasing mistakes experienced substantial disposition effects; as such, they were eager to realize gains early, but reluctant to do so with losses (Frydman & Camerer, 2016, p. 5; Statman, 2019, p. 56).

Du, Niessen, and Odean (2019) found that pride seeking caused some mutual fund managers to repurchase specific stocks, while regret aversion resulted in them being unwilling to purchase them (p. 1). On average, the probability of a manager repurchasing stocks is 17% greater if the stocks were sold earlier for a profit resulting in pride, as opposed to a loss that inflicted regret; the lesson: seeking pride and avoiding regret harms returns as winners who were repurchased underperform repurchased losers by an average of 5% per annum (Du, Niessen, & Odean, 2019, p. 1).

3.2.7 Herding and Conformity

Herding is one of the more common phenomena of distorted rational behavior, one that is equally affecting retail investors and professionals (Spindler, 2011, p. 324; Shiller 2000, p. 149). Since individuals tend to stick to the "mainstream," as represented by a peer group/leader, they often overlook other signs and indicators, which under rational behavior, would drive them towards an entirely different evaluation of the actual situation (Spindler, 2011, p. 324). Individuals have a natural tendency of simplifying complex processes of decision-making, which causes them to merely copy others' decisions; the motive is that a sense of security is experienced by the individual with respect to having chosen a path already undertaken by others, this is called the conformity effect (Spindler, 2011, p. 324).

Furthermore, principal-agent concerns are significantly impacted by herding behavior, since careers and bonuses of intermediaries are linked to their performance relative to their reference peer group members; therefore, a strong incentive is prevalent for not straying away from mainstream thinking (Scharfstein & Stein, 1990, p. 465). The financial crisis demonstrated how financial institutions on a global scale decided to join in on the bandwagon of investing in asset-backed securities to ensure that they do not miss out on promising performance and to justify to shareholders who might question why they did not follow the general trends (Spindler, 2011, p. 325).

3.3 *Efficient v. Irrational*

In 2013 Professor Eugene Fama of the University of Chicago and Professor Robert Schiller of Yale University shared the Nobel Memorial Prize in Economic Sciences; their research contribution into the movement of asset prices like stocks, bonds and real estate have laid the foundation for several financial topics (Nobel Prize, 2013). However, their findings were entirely opposing; how could two men share the same Nobel Prize with radically conflicting views on what moves asset prices? Most would agree that people exhibit irrational tendencies and that sometimes those tendencies impact how they behave in markets; however, the divide between behavioralists and market efficiency theorists is whether these tendencies impact overall market prices, and if so, can these anomalies be exploited to consistently outperform the market benchmark (Malkiel, 2003, p. 6).

Eugene Fama (1970) conceptualized the Efficient Markets Hypothesis (EMH) in which he asserts that prices rationally reflect all available information as information is publicly disseminated market participants quickly takes that information and move the price of any given asset towards its efficient equilibrium (p. 383). The implication is that if markets behaved that efficiently it would be nearly impossible to find a consistent way of exploiting anomalies to beat the market. Robert Schiller's (1981) counterpoint argument to EMH was by looking into the irrational price action activity in dividend-yielding stocks (p. 421). Schiller (1981) questioned why there was such irrational excess in range and volatility in these stocks prices when the dividend yields were already known; if people are valuating stocks based on discounting future cash flows, then why are price fluctuations so vastly dislocated from the "minimal dividend fluctuation" (p. 421)? He asserts that these anomalies could not be anything other than irrational/emotional participation (Schiller, 1981, p. 422). Schiller is quoted claiming that "the assertion stock prices were rational was one of the most remarkable errors in the history of economic thought. Mass psychology may well be the dominant cause of movements in the price of the aggregate stock market" (Appelbaum, 2013, para.21).

A classic example of price movement irrationality is demonstrated by Thaler in a debate against Fama; Thaler demonstrated how in 2012 when the Cuban news aired that President Obama was going to normalize relationship with Cuba the market was rushing to invest in Cuban related assets with one particular closed-end fund going by the ticker "CUBA" surging in price (Chicago Booth Review, 2016). The herd found that ticker and piled in, biding up the price to a point where its price was significantly worth more than the net asset value of that fund, ironically, that fund had absolutely nothing to do with Cuba the Country (Chicago Booth Review, 2016).

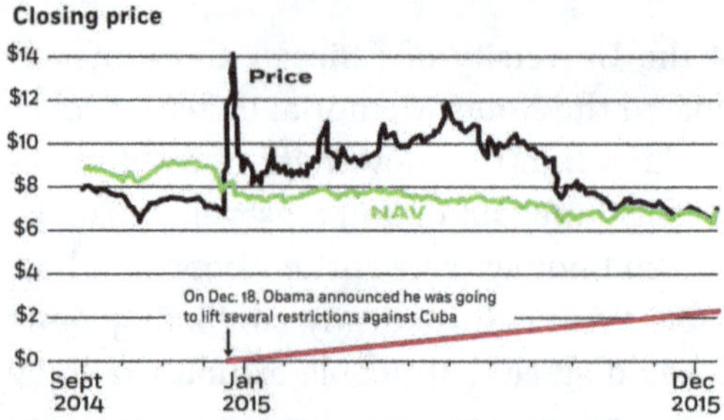

FIGURE 3 CUBA price chart
CHICAGO BOOTH REVIEW, 2016

A more recent example from last year is the confusion between the ticker for Zoom Communication and Zoom Technologies. "Zoom, the popular video chat platform trades under the Ticker 'ZM'. The Ticker 'Zoom' however belongs to a Chinese company that makes parts for mobile devices. The accidental purchase of the wrong Zoom shares rocketed the price of the lesser-known company up by 1800%. Subsequently, the SEC stepped in and removed Zoom from the stock market" (McGrath, 2020, para.6). It would be fascinating to study how much due diligence or simple information gathering was conducted by investors before buying the wrong stock. The price action in Figures three and four neatly demonstrate a flaw in EMH where it is not just the available information that is demonstrated in price movements, but perhaps human folly as well. So, are markets efficient or are they driven by emotion? Perhaps the symbolism of a shared Noble prize speaks for itself in this continual debate.

3.4 *Behavioral Critique*

There is substantial discourse among economists regarding the validity of behavioral findings; the critics believe the behavioral approach is excessively unstructured, thereby permitting essentially any anomaly to be explained through a combination of irrationalities selected from a list of behavioral errors (Bodie, 2009, p. 399). These critics want to view a consistent or unified behavioral theory for explaining behavioral anomalies in markets (Bodie, 2009, p. 399).

Fama (1998) is specifically unconvinced that the literature related to anomalies is a persuading counter to the efficient market hypothesis (p. 283). It is noted by Fama (1998) that the anomalies are not in line with their support for one kind of irrationality visa via others (p. 283). What is meant is that while some experiments document correction anomalies (in line with overreaction), continuances of abnormal returns are documented by others (in line with underreaction) (Bodie, 2009, p. 399). Furthermore, the statistical significance of several such

FIGURE 4 ZM VS ZOOM price chart
MCGRATH, 2020

findings is difficult to justify; even minute errors when selecting a benchmark against which returns are compared can add up to significant superficial anomalies in long-term returns (Fama, 1998, p. 283; Bodie, 2009, p. 399).

The behavioral school of thought is well taken when it comes to nullifying assumptions of absolute rationality in decision-making, though the degree to which limited rationality impacts the market continues to remain controversial (Bodie, 2009, p. 400). Ironically, insights of behavioral finance point towards some of the same recommendations promoted by advocates of the EMH; for instance, one simple way to sidestep some major behavioral errors involves investing into passive indexed strategies (Bodie, 2009, p. 400). It would appear that only a few talented managers can consistently beat passive index investing over the long haul and as such, the recommendation holds regardless of whether one is a behavioralist or EMH supporter (Bodie, 2009, p. 400).

3.5 *Outlook*

As shown in this chapter, research into behavioral finance highlights that the cognitive capacity of individuals is limited with respect to information processing and that typically, emotional and motivational aspects are the influential factors in our decision making; essentially, we are unable to act completely rational even if we wanted. With our bounded rationality, errors such as information and choice overload hamper our information processing abilities. To cope with such a situation, we use biases and heuristics to ease our decision constraints. Unfortunately, these biases can cause us to disregard or dismiss important information regarding risks. Instead, we tend to focus on the information that is readily available and is framed most appealingly. We seem to be highly seduced to replicate the decisions of other people as opposed to weighing our decisions on our personal needs and situation. As a result of all this, implicitly people wouldn't be able or explicitly wouldn't want to make decisions based on information alone. Within this context, disclosure cannot be the primary criterion for effective investor protection. As shall be further be discussed in the following chapters, findings from behavioral finance pose a major regulatory challenge for which an effective and sustainable solution is still lacking.

4 Critical Reflection of EU Investor Protection Frameworks

The fundamental assumptions of market participants' rational behavior and the instruments required for overcoming possible asymmetry of information are deep-seated in EU regulatory reasoning; economists typically see regulations as a way to rectify (and overcome) market failures, and amongst the more used tools in investor protection frameworks concentrate on information disclosure in general (Moloney, 2008, p. 92; Spindler, 2011, p. 318).

It is undeniable that while professional market participants, including banks and other financial intermediaries are capable of evaluating complex market and financial data to determine the quality of financial products, typically, retail investors are not equally skilled in their assessment of such complex data (Spindler, 2011, p. 318). As opposed to a tangible asset, it is not possible for an investor to tangibly check a financial product "condition" and thus they are challenged to forecast both its actual and future value; furthermore, it takes excessive time and effort for a retail client to seek and evaluate the information that is available (Camerer et al., 1989, p. 1232). Bewilderingly, on a European level, legislators still maintain the notion that effective investor protection can be achieved by the provision of an all-encompassing disclosure framework (Ben-Shahar & Schneider, 2010, p. 650; Spindler, 2011, p. 319).

In Support of Kammel's (2015) concept of the regulatory pendulum (p. 19), we can witness financial markets' deregulation, which initiated in the 1980s, and was justified from the perspective that markets are largely efficient and rational; complacence regarding increasing prices of homes in the 2000s also reflected the approach that prices are innately rational (Appelbaum, 2013, para.11). However, the severe implications of the financial crisis swung the pendulum towards stricter control over various sectors of financial regulation, including banking supervisory regulations (Weiss & Kammel, 2015, p. 25). Apart from stronger supervisory regulations, legal discussions were also placing investor protection on the agenda, specifically questioning if conventional means and instruments are adequate to avoid similar problems in the future (Spindler, 2011, p. 319). Thus, it is unsurprising that in the aftermath of the crisis, Mr. Shiller's work, along with other advocates of behavioral finance have been influential voices in reshaping our understanding of investor behavior (Appelbaum, 2013, para.11) and the possible implications it has on financial regulation (Kammel, 2015, p. 4).

This study has extensively discussed how findings from behavioral finance conflict with traditional economic and legal assumptions. With that in mind, this subsequent chapter shall critically examine EU regulatory frameworks, particularly the utility of mandated disclosures as tools for investor protection. Prior to such an examination, the chapter shall provide a few ongoing red threats and informational asymmetries that pose a looming challenge over effective investor protection efforts.

4.1 *Red Threats*

4.1.1 Incentive Systems

For professionals, the short-term oriented thinking that could be witnessed prior to the crisis was primarily instigated by inducements systems linked to short-term benchmarking metrics (Swedberg, 2010, p. 84). Such systems did not facilitate the sharing of losses but did so for gains, thereby instilling a short-term risk-taking bias into its participants (Spindler, 2011, p. 324). The marketing and selling of financial products to retail investors are similarly conducted with misaligned incentive consideration; as intermediaries seek to bolster their commission fees, they are incentivized to recommend specific products (with higher kickbacks) to their clients, thereby disregarding their fiduciary duties of consulting their client in an objective manner (Swedberg, 2010, p. 79).

A key factor leading up to the GFC was the inability of professional intermediaries to understand the systemic risks building up as a result of increased issuance of asset-backed certificates; furthermore, long-term implications were underestimated, while the short-term orientation thinking combined with the contagion herding risks were left ignored up until the start of the financial crisis (Swedberg, 2010, p. 86). But these faults cannot be narrowed down as irrational behavior, since they were a result of the system's dysfunction; contrastingly, it was a rational decision made by professionals motivated by a short-term oriented incentive system (Spindler, 2011, p. 325). As such, a lurking threat to financial stability and investor protection lies not only in the conventional assumptions of rationality in legal deliberation but in the current pitfalls of risk management, supervision and inducements policies of financial institutions.

4.1.2 Commission-Free Brokers and Gamification

There is a clear shift in the industry geared towards commission-free brokerages with a business model designed to profit from higher-order flows, thus turning their "users" into a monetized "product" to be sold to market makers (Wang, 2021, p. 50). These brokerages face a perverse incentive and conflict of interest as they are incentivized to send their clients' order flows to market makers that pay them the most for the flow rather than to firms that might provide the best execution (Wang, 2021, p. 51).

It is widely known by now that most retail investors lose money and that frequent trading results in poor performance (Barber & Odean, 2013, p. 5). However, these commission-free brokers such as Robinhood have invested heavily into behavioral research to increase their trading activity using gaming design elements to encourage (nudge) more frequent trading from their users, thus profiting from each order flow (Van der Heide & Želinský, 2021, p. 2). How would they dispute this clear conflict of interest with their clients' interests for sustainable capital appreciation if they fail to warn them of the undisputed danger of frequent trading?

Some observable examples of the gamification nudges that encourage frequent activity are: on signup users receive a digital scratch-off with one free stock, constant push notification of top 10 hot stocks and confetti graphics when orders are filled (Wursthorn & Choi, 2021, para.3). These gamification features pose a serious hazard for inexperienced investors; to be clear these elements are designed to manipulate retail investors to trade more for the benefit of the broker at their expanse. Securities law has legitimate causes for action in this regard, from conflicts of interests, duty in best execution, and perhaps even breach of fiduciary duty by nudging inexperienced investors to trade more (Wang, 2021, p. 52). How could traditional forms of investor protection, such as disclosure, possibly cope with brokerages who tacitly exploit the behavioral errors that endanger investors in the first place?

4.1.3 Speculative Bubbles

Former Fed Chairman Alan Greenspan stated that the dot-com boom was "irrational exuberance," his evaluation eventually came to fruition: by October 2002, the value of NASDAQ declined to less than one-fourth of its highs that were attained just 2½ years prior (Ferguson, 2008, p. 124). This is an interesting case for proponents of the behavioral school, as it exemplifies a market that was affected by irrational sentiments of investors (Bodie, 2009, p. 398). In line with behavioral patterns, with the development of the dot-com boom, the rally began to feed on itself, and investors become particularly overconfident regarding their investment prowess and were eager to deduce short-range patterns (representativeness) and predict them as the outcomes of distant future (Bodie, 2009, p. 398). Five years after that, there was an emergence of another bubble taking to form of derivatives secured to rising housing prices; similar to the dot-com bubble, speculative demand was accelerated by the potential for further increase in prices (Ferguson, 2008, p. 125). Unsurprisingly, the demand for housing at such prices stalled before eventually crashing, thereby causing the worst financial crisis in 75 years (Bodie, 2009, p. 398).

It is easy to identify bubbles in hindsight, however, when they are still underway, it is unclear if the market is behaving irrationally; during the dot-com bubble, several financial commentators justified the boom as in line with the positive forecasts for the "new economy" (Bodie, 2009, p. 398). However, according to other observers, the dot-com boom showed signs of irrationality; for instance, firms that add ".com" at the end of their names within this period resulted in a significant stock price increase (Cooper, Dimitrov & Rau, 2001, p. 2371). The same could be hypothesized of firms who recently added the word "blockchain" to their names.

Stories associated with financial excess such as the dot-com craze, function as warnings to new and old investors, specifically for retail investors whose life savings are on the line. Speculative markets will always be prevalent where the old rules seem to not apply; the signs are usually evident and follow a pattern: from technological or financial "displacement," extreme credit use, forgetfulness of the last bubble, and new surges of naive investors who view the markets as a get rich quick scheme (Ferguson, 2008, p. 121). In these cases, it would be wise to guard one's wallet and heed John Templeton's famed warning "The four most expensive words in the English language are: this time, it's different" (Bernstein, 2002, p. 152).

4.1.4 Risk and Uncertainty

Financial history has illustrated many bubbles and busts, new highs and feared lows, short-term shocks and devastating crashes (Ferguson, 2008, p. 342; Neal, 2000, p. 317). According to Barro's (2005) study conducted on the data available on GDP and consumption since 1870, there were a total of 148 crises wherein a country underwent a cumulative fall in GDP of a minimum of 10% and 87 crises wherein there was a substantial decline in consumption, indicating a possibility of financial disaster of approximately 3.6% each year (p. 831; Ferguson, 2008, p. 342).

Even in our current technologically advanced world with our sophisticated tools and analytical prowess, we remain vulnerable to the next unknown crisis; despite our ingenuity, we continue to get "fooled by randomness" (Taleb, 2005, p. 4) with "black swans" surprising us when we least expect them (Taleb, 2007,

p. 20). Unfraternally, much of the future is uncertain and thus, its risk is incalculable (Taleb, 2007, p. 29). As Frank Knight (1921) states, "uncertainty must be taken in a sense radically distinct from the familiar notion of risk, from which it has never been properly separated" (p. 197). With respect to uncertain knowledge, Keynes (1937) stated:

> I do not mean merely to distinguish what is known for certain from what is only probable. Even the weather is only moderately uncertain. The sense in which I am using the term is that in which the prospect of a European war is uncertain, or the rate of interest twenty years hence … About these matters there is no scientific basis on which to form any calculable probability whatever. We simply do not know. (p. 213)

Later, Keynes (1937) went on and hypothesized regarding how investors, in these uncertain circumstances, manage to behave in a way that saves face as "rational economic men":

> We assume that the present is a much more serviceable guide to the future than a candid examination of past experience would show it to have been hitherto. We assume that the existing state of opinion as expressed in prices and the character of existing output is based on a correct summing up of future prospects. Knowing that our own individual judgment is worthless, we endeavor to fall back on the judgment of the rest of the world which is perhaps better informed. That is, we endeavor to conform with the behavior of the majority or the average. (p. 214)

Keynes rightly interpreted an intrinsic characteristic of investor behavior, as it is undeniable that human behaviors play a crucial part in the financial system's instability; we can witness this in ourselves and our institutions as we rapidly veer from euphoria to despair combined with our inability to remain secured against 'tail risk' and our constant failure to learn from our history (Ferguson, 2008, p. 344). Considering this discussion, one must wonder if traditional tools of investor protection are fit for purpose. As such, the following subchapters will critically analyze some of the EU's investor protection frameworks and interpret their utility from the perspective of retail investors.

4.2 *Investor Protection and Transparency*

The GFC revealed that investor protection and the stability of the financial institutions go hand in hand; a systemic failure of a financial institution does not only damage the financial sector but to a larger extent the economy which in turn hurts the depositors and investors the hardest (Plato-Shinar, 2015,

p. 223). Therefore, it needs to be shown that investor protection depends on the stability of the financial institution, and to an extent the financial institutions depend on the welfare of its investors, leading to the point that if the investors lose their trust in the system a cascading effect will surely occur. To build and maintain investors' trust in the system various transparency tools such as mandated disclosure are viewed as key to such a cause.

Transparency is commonly regarded as a fundamental principle, one in which enables the public to gain informative insight into the structures and operations of a given entity (Hood & Heald, 2006, p. 26). In Western cultures, transparency and its regulation is considered to be a self-evident good much like free speech and privacy rights (Etzioni, 2010, p. 1). Organizations and governments have ascended this principle to the point of which it is regarded as "holier-than-thou" (Hood, 2006, p. 9). Ripken (2006) expands on this: "Respect for individual autonomy, responsibility, and decision-making is deeply entrenched in our culture and law ... We believe that people can order their own economic affairs and, given sufficient information, can make their own personal assessments of the risks and benefits of transactions" (p. 195). Ripken (2006) continues by mentioning that "disclosure promotes fairness and empowers the investor with information to make smart investment choices" (p. 153). As such, it is no wonder that on both the national and supernational levels product information is regarded as a key building block for investor protection (Colaert, 2017, p. 2).

The traditional ideal of the "information paradigm" has long been viewed as being one of the pillars of investor protection solutions; however, conflicting opinions regarding aspects of the paradigm have led to intense criticism over the cost/value of transparency in the years following the GFC, thus damaging investor confidence in financial transparency and the system as a whole (Colaert, 2017, p. 2). To reiterate, the term "information paradigm" assumes that investors are in a position to make prudent financial decisions based on the knowledge attained from disclosures of financial institutions, being fully aware of the risks involved (Colaert, 2017, p. 2). In order to mitigate market failure due to informational asymmetry, enhancing transparency empowers market participants in making better informed financial decisions for themselves (Colaert, 2017, p. 3).

For the public selling of financial products, the information paradigm within the context of investor protection is best demonstrated by means of obligatory prospectus requirements; the prospectus aim is in providing the investor with viable information from the issuer, these documents have long been harmonized by EU member states (Coleart, 2017, p. 4). Lai, Liu and Wang (2014), found that such disclosures help in reducing information asymmetry in addition to improving market efficiency by inducing executives to act in their shareholder's best interest (p. 308). Article 7 of the currently in force Prospectus Regulation (EU) 2017/1129 perceives a strong bond between informed investors and market efficiency:

> The aim of this Regulation is to ensure investor protection and market efficiency, while enhancing the internal market for capital. The provision of information which, according to the nature of the issuer and of the securities, is necessary to enable investors to make an informed investment decision ensures, together with rules on the conduct of business, the protection of investors. Moreover, such information provides an effective means of increasing confidence in securities and thus of contributing to the proper functioning and development of securities markets. (p. 168/13)

There's no argument that fair and competitive market dynamics have been positively driven by greater transparency. Specifically, information about costs is a core attribute for differentiation in buying decisions in the context of mutual funds. The fact that there are plenty of passive products which are being offered at a lower cost increases the pressure on active managers to make sure that the higher costs can be justified. However, this paper is geared more towards issues stemming from disclosures utility in enabling informed financial decisions. As former FED Chair, Alan Greenspan (2003) has suggested, any potential issues with transparency are linked to issues with disclosure; his distinction of the two are as follows:

> In the minds of some, public disclosure and transparency are interchangeable. But they are not. Transparency implies that information allows an understanding of a firm's exposures and risks without distortion. The goal of improved transparency thus represents a higher bar than the goal of improved disclosures. Transparency challenges market participants not only to provide information but also to place that information in a context that makes it meaningful. (Greenspan, 2003, p. 12)

Greenspan's remarks suggest that transparency through the mandated provision of a firm's financial information does not necessarily translate towards improved transparency, at least not in the sense of added utility to the broader investor pool. This essentially leads to complex issues of how to best present disclosures that would have added utility without omitting critical information. The following subchapters will further discuss such complexities and challenges that emerge from mandated disclosures.

4.3 *The Challenge of Disclosures and the Information Paradigm*

In the aftermath of the GFC financial regulators directed their collective efforts towards enhancing disclosures that firms make with respect to their risk exposures, specifically those related to derivatives (Davies & Green, 2013, p. 41). Public authorities, as well as private-sector working groups suggested measures for improving market discipline by various forms of enhancing public disclosures; however, these efforts led to mixed results (Davies & Green, 2013, p. 41). It is true that we came a long way in the expansion of the volume of information that is publicly disclosed and associated with risk exposures; however, the more complex question is if this increased volume has led to improvements in market discipline?

Disclosure challenges firms to pose information that precisely highlights risks; currently, a lot of disclosure falls short of such demanding goals (Greenspan, 2003, p. 3). Though there is significant room for progress with respect to disclosures, the limitations to achieving it should not be underestimated. Firms continue to struggle with the selection and presentation of data in a meaningful way; annual reports of big institutions reflect these challenges, as they typically surpass one hundred pages with enormous pressures to comply with constant changes to mandated requirements (Greenspan, 2003, p. 3). The critical issue here is that transparency mandates the dissemination of disclosure, but does not supervise over the effective communication with its intended audience (O'Neal, 2006, p. 81). To address this challenge, industry executives and leaders of public policy must remain focused on "the ultimate goal, a clear understanding of a firm's activities that fosters market discipline" (Flannery, 1996, p. 1357).

Etzioni (2010) explains that "the critical question is whether transparency constitutes a reliable mechanism of promoting good governance and sound markets under most circumstances—or whether it is a rather weak means that itself relies on other forms of guidance and can supplement regulation but not serve a main form of guidance" (p. 3). Within this context, transparency functions as a relatively soft regulatory measure, as aligning with its requirements is not as restrictive for producer and consumer choice, when compared to other forms of regulations (Etzioni, 2010, p. 10). Regardless, for it to work, investors must still be able to process and assimilate such information.

This does not suggest that offering transparency where it is limited does not offer value, instead, that in and of itself it is typically not enough to meet the high goals set for it (Etzioni, 2010, p. 10). In essence, there is room to enhance further support of disclosure in tandem with an amendment towards intermediary supervision; however, it is still insufficient protection when transactional costs of the information have diminishing returns. (Etzioni, 2010, p. 16). As such, the following segment ties in with examining this lack of utility from a retail perspective.

4.4 *Caveats in Market Mechanism and Regulatory Intervention*

4.4.1 Investor Behavior

The importance of transparency is undeniable, though its intended effect is somewhat overcome by a multitude of behavioral biases and legal constraints. As discussed in the prior chapter, the field of behavioral finance reveals major gaps in the information paradigm. There is a surplus of biases and psychological heuristics that negatively impact the desired effects of which financial transparency aims to achieve. It goes so far as even when provided with a simplified summarized version of complex information, the information asymmetry does not necessarily improve, on the contrary, investors are more likely to ignore or misinterpret that too (Colaert, 2017, p. 5).

Behavioral economists, Amos Tversky and Daniel Kahneman (1974) revealed this more than four decades ago when they found that very often even simple information is improperly processed by the public; this is primarily due to various embedded heuristics and systematic cognitive biases (p. 33). Recent studies conducted by Chicago Booth's Initiative on Global Markets found that consumer behavior to disclosure is not dependent on the information itself, but rather by the individual's interpretation of the information and in their ability to make use of it (Prat, 2005, p. 93; Gold, 2016, para.5). Chicago Booth's Professor Urminsky believes that "disclosure alone doesn't always have beneficial effects ... I don't think disclosure is a cure-all" (Gold, 2016, para.6). Accordingly, to provide optimal transparency to the public, policy makers must consider the information received by consumers, as well as how and if they can use it.

4.4.2 Rating Agencies

There are various forms of packaged information available to an investor when selecting financial products; for instance, mutual fund ratings issued by specialized rating agencies such as Moodie's, S&P or Morningstar provide relevant financial information in a condensed fashion (Oehler & Wendt, 2017, p. 186). Such ratings add up relevant information in an attempt to help with the decision-making process; ill-advisedly, those using mutual fund ratings to determine where to invest, either implicitly or explicitly presume that these ratings denote information pertaining to future mutual fund performance (Oehler & Wendt, 2017, p. 186). Initially, mutual fund ratings seem easily comprehensible; but these ratings do not elaborate on relevant information regarding some crucial characteristics of mutual funds (Oehler & Wendt, 2017, p. 186).

As claimed by Oehler and Wendt (2017), mutual fund ratings do not adequately differentiate high-quality funds with respect to a superior risk-return relationship from lesser caliber funds (p. 187). Hence, such ratings are ambiguous as they provide unclear information regarding the characteristics of the product and the implications of investing in them; as such, investors, specifically retail investors, do not enjoy significant benefits from mutual fund ratings when making decisions, as they do not fulfill an essential informational requirement (Oehler & Wendt, 2017, p. 186). McDonald and Rietz (2018) further found that the simple ordinal scale rating figure, in and of itself and excluding all additional contextual information, has a substantial influence on investment decisions and has shown to harm performance (p. 1). It is also argued that comparability between products categories is arbitrary since the rating process is usually conducted in a nontransparent manner nor would it be understandable for people external to the rating agencies which also further negatively impacts the verifiability of such ratings (McDonald & Rietz, 2014, p. 2).

Due largely in part to their failure during the financial crisis, there has been a decline in rating agencies' credibility, as among other things they were held responsible for the market's breakdown (Spindler, 2011, p. 318). One cause for this decline in credibility stems from the inherent conflict of interests these rating agencies find themselves in; the call for an estimation that is objective and realistic is pertinent, however, one must remember that these agencies are hired by the issuers, thus enabling the issuer to leverage the situation to their advantage (Spindler, 2011, p. 318). A negative evaluation or a downgrading typically results in contrary effects, as a downgrade could stimulate certain covenants or other obligations that are conditional in nature (Covitz & Harrison, 2003, p. 6). Furthermore, rating agencies attempted to enter into markets wherein the mechanisms were ambiguous to them—thereby, resulting in conventional reputational mechanisms which did function properly (Goodhart 2008, p. 338; Spindler, 2011, p. 318).

4.4.3 Financial Intermediaries

As was discussed previously regarding the cost/utility of processing information, the same argument can be made for the utility in determining which intermediary is the best provider of information for oneself? Each intermediary brings with it a slew of differences regarding access to primary information and market outlook; the analysts at these firms differ in training, skill and in their diverse biased assumptions (Etzioni, 2010, p. 12). It goes to show that if an investor is already challenged with first-order information, the volume of the challenge is exacerbated when dealing with intermediaries (second order) "processed" information.

Etzioni's (2010) argument directly aligns with this paper's conceptual model, (see figure 1) regarding the caveat of mediated information processed through financial intermediaries. Strathern (2000) anthropologic study further address this phenomenon of mediated disclosure and points towards an infinite regression to higher claims to transparency, exacerbated by the users' refusal to recognize the inherent bias in what is raveled freely (p. 310). His argument expands on the idea that there is no such thing as "raw data", as it is always mediated in some form or another in becoming "produced data" by the time it's publicly disseminated (Strathern, 2000, p. 310). This obviously adds another layer of ambiguity and complexity for the investor who must now interpret mediated and at times biased information. It seems ironic that transparency in and of itself could become a tool of concealment.

4.4.4 Key Information Documents

Several past and continually updated EU directives have attempted to mitigate the negative effects of information overload and irrational biases; from UCITS simplified prospectus which inspired the currently in force Regulation (EU) No 1286/2014 that requires the use of a "Key Investor Document" (KID) for all "Packaged Retail Investment and Insurance Based Investment Products" (PRIIPS) (Colaert, 2017, p. 8). The KID requirement is a clear example of contemporary actions taken by European legislation in its efforts to mitigate information asymmetries in the financial markets. Article 6 of the aforementioned regulations elaborates as follows:

> The key information document shall be drawn up as a short document written in a concise manner and of a maximum of three sides of A4-sized paper when printed, which promotes comparability. It shall: (a) be presented and laid out in a way that is easy to read, using characters of readable size; (b) focus on the key information that retail investors need; (c) be clearly expressed and written in language and a style that communicate in a way that facilitates the understanding of the information, in particular, in language that is clear, succinct and comprehensible. (EU No 1286/2014, p. 5)

However, a number of studies demonstrate that actual KIDS usually do not accurately portray critical characteristics of financial products; particularly, the presentation and comparability of risks remains inadequate (Oehler, Höfer

& Wendt, 2014, p. 115; Godwin & Ramsay, 2015, p. 54). When it comes to product comparability, investors and intermediaries face a serious obstacle. As of yet, there is no standardized way to fairly present the differentiated characteristics between financial products, such as linearly structured mutual fund products and nonlinear insurance-linked structured products; although often being very similar in their objective, these products differ in their characteristics and regulatory requirement (Oehler & Wendt, 2017, p. 187). Apart from this, KIDs usually do not contain information regarding the fit of the products based on the financial needs of the investor (Oehler & Wendt, 2017, p. 187).

With respect to the admirable objectives of the PRIIP KID, a daunting commissioned study on the subject revealed that a substantial number of retail investors fail to draw correct deductions from the information provided by the finest selection of KID samples (MARKT/2014/060/G, 2015, p. 198). The motivation for this experimental study was to examine the comprehension effectiveness of the new KID regulation on retail investors; a regulation which requires the KID to be in a short, standardized and in a consumer-friendly format when presented to potential retail investors interested in buying PRIIPs (MARKT/2014/060/G, 2015, p. 3).

Some of the main questions asked of the study group after they reviewed the sample KIDs were: "What is this investment? What are the risks and what could I get in return? What are the costs? How long should I hold it and can I take money out early? How can I complain (MARKT/2014/060/G, 2015, p. 3)?" The findings reviled that of the 6,954 tested participants from across the EU, a substantial proportion had difficulties in comprehending concepts such as capital guarantees, various performance scenarios, elements of multi-option products, and difficulties in comprehending that the costs were estimations and not exact figures (MARKT/2014/060/G, 2015, p. 198). Even if performance scenarios would be accurate, can we expect retail clients to understand that, for example, the 12 performance scenarios shown are only an indication of a range of return expectations, not to mention that they are not even probability weighted. In addition, with regards to processing the information of the already simplified KID, the experiment reviled that the amount of information was in some cases, detrimental for comprehension of key elements (MARKT/2014/060/G, 2015, p. 199).

4.5 *MiFID II Critical Analysis*

On the European front, In order to strengthen capital markets in the aftermath of the financial crisis, in July 2014 the European Commission initiated the revised Markets in Financial Instruments Directive (MiFID II), the associated Markets in Financial Instruments Regulation (MIFIR) as well as the Regulation on Key Information Documents for Packaged Retail and Insurance-based

Investment Products (PRIIPS KID), all of which were finally implemented by January 2018 (Paul, Schröder, & Schumacher, 2019, p. 2). MiFID II is still considered to be amongst one of the most important European financial directives; a directive that unsurprisingly takes the approach of focusing on enhancing disclosure requirements as one of its primary directives (Springer, 2011, p. 319).

MiFID II "mandates investment firms to offer clients or even potential clients with accurate information pertaining to the firm and its services, financial instruments" (EU No 2014/65, Art.24), as well as planned investment strategies, by providing appropriate guidance regarding the investments and associated risks, or when it comes to "particular investment strategies, execution venues, costs and associated charges" (EU No 2014/65, Art.24). Springer (2011) states that "these duties are explicitly aimed at providing clients an insight view into the nature and risks of the investment service and of the specific type of financial instrument that is being offered. Thus, clients shall be provided with a fully informed basis to take investment decisions" (p. 319).

A lot of resources were expended by EU and overseas companies to align their operations with MiFID II and yet while still in its early stages, the European Fund and Asset Management Association (ESMA) is already proposing amendments in response to broad criticism from the industry (Klimesch & Klar, 2020, para.2). In a 2019 conference, ESMA's Chair, Steven Maijoor, reminded people of the great strides MiFID II has achieved for market transparency and cost disclosures (Klimesch & Klar, 2020, para.4). However, not all market participants agree, voicing concerns of increasing expenses, loopholes and inconsistencies (Klimesch & Klar, 2020, para.5). They cite several areas ripe for review and change including examining the effects of cost disclosures and transparency of fees, examining the impact of unbundling research, especially in coverage "over smaller listed companies, as many believe coverage has weakened dramatically, and changes are needed to provide incentives to restore it" (Klimesch & Klar, 2020, para.6). The subsequent section will briefly elaborate on some of these key concerns.

4.5.1 Suitability and Appropriateness

As part of the onboarding process, firms who offer investment advice are obliged to conduct and document a suitability and appropriateness test on behalf of their prospecting clients (Colaert, 2017, p. 13); these suitability checks have been further bolstered under MiFID II stipulating:

> The investment firm shall obtain the necessary information regarding the client's or potential client's knowledge and experience in the investment field relevant to the specific type of product or service, that person's

> financial situation including his ability to bear losses, and his investment objectives including his risk tolerance so as to enable the investment firm to recommend to the client or potential client the investment services and financial instruments that are suitable for him and, in particular, are in accordance with his risk tolerance and ability to bear losses. (EU No 2014/65, Art.25)

It would be intriguing to know how such risk tolerance claims can be genuinely determined. It's easy to be overconfident during a bull market, but will these clients' statements regarding their ability to bear losses remain true during a 30% drawdown or a protracted bear market? MiFID also attempts to inform investors throughout their investment life cycle by requiring advisors (within 24 hours) to report if a 10% portfolio drop has accrued within the current quarter. However, within the context of behavioral judgment this rule could be argued to be counterproductive as it has the potential to cause panic selling during a down market. "l'histoire se répète" is a common phrase during every market crisis where we can large volume of withdrawals near bottoms. Any credible advisor would recommend strongly against such a move as stepping away at the lows rather than just waiting a few years for the market to correct could hurt performance. The more logical approach would be to have it both ways, a notification whenever one's portfolio is down 10% or up 10% for the quarter; this would teach people that volatility is not necessarily a bad thing in the long run, but detrimental if given credence in the short term.

4.5.2 Product Restriction

Wealth managers and financial advisers allow their clients the possibility to self-advice; this execution-only service entails that these "advisory firms" merely execute orders without oversight or prudential advice, thus leading to a potentially misleading understanding of the term "advisory" (Weiss, & Kammel, 2015, p. 287). More pertinent, this execution-only option is restricted to products that are non-complex, as complex products are believed as too risky for retail clients to handle (Deloitte, 2014, p. 7).

Counterintuitively, structured UCITS funds (Undertakings for the Collective Investment in Transferable Securities) which currently adhere to all of "ESMA's Technical Advice" are deemed as complex products (ESMA, 2014/1569, p. 157); these products were specifically designed for retail investors with the aim of mitigating full market risks though capital protection guarantees (Deloitte, 2014, p. 7). Curiously, products deemed as "non-complex" and permitted to be sold to execution-only clients, such as equity mutual funds, expose investors to full market risks and provide an inferior anticipated outcome; as such, retail clients who wish to directly deploy their savings into "complex" UCITS fund must first seek professional financial advice and incur the costs involved (Deloitte, 2014, p. 7).

> The millions of European individuals who allocate their savings to lottery tickets do so without advice, those wishing to invest in a structured/capital protected UCITS will need to seek professional opinion. Here the regulation appears to seek to play the role of deciding for investors what they are able or unable to understand, and commits the cardinal fallacy of confusing complexity with risk. (Deloitte, 2014, p. 5)

4.5.3 Unbundling Research

MiFID II mandates asset managers to 'unbundle' costs of research from the total sums that the investors are charged; the regulatory aim for this was to "increase transparency" on hidden costs (Lang, Pinto & Sul, 2019, p. 1). Unreasonably, regulators did not successfully ensure that the industry was prepared for this and other changes imposed by the rapid implementation of MiFID II (Robinson, 2017, para.2). The guidelines outlined were neither clear or concise, and each financial institution had to pay for the expenses of seeking help from teams of compliance professionals to understand these new regulatory requirements (Lang, Pinto & Sul, 2019, p. 6). Consequentially and unintentionally, the European financial markets have seen a massive "plunge by as much as 20% in the volume and breadth of research produced since the implementation of MiFID II" (Lee, 2019, para.3).

By reducing their research expenses, firms have significantly decreased the total number of analysts employed; as a result, this affected the volume of research that was conducted on smaller stocks as the analysts who remained focused on the largest stocks (Lee, 2019, para.12). Unbundling was not meant to cause such effects; these policies have unfairly disadvantaged smaller EU firms. While clients were fussing over the high costs of research, many larger players chose to absorb these costs as opposed to passing them on to their clients; however, small and medium-sized enterprises (SME's) cannot afford to do as such, resulting in loss of business to the bigger players (Lee, 2019, para.12). Long-term, these policies will harm competition as they apply pressure for further consolidation in the financial industry (Lee, 2019, para.3).

4.6 *Outlook*

This paper views disclosure utility for a retail investor as an auxiliary and unnecessary legal liability proceeding. Much like the concept of an app's end-user agreement that goes largely unread, so is probably true of financial disclosure.

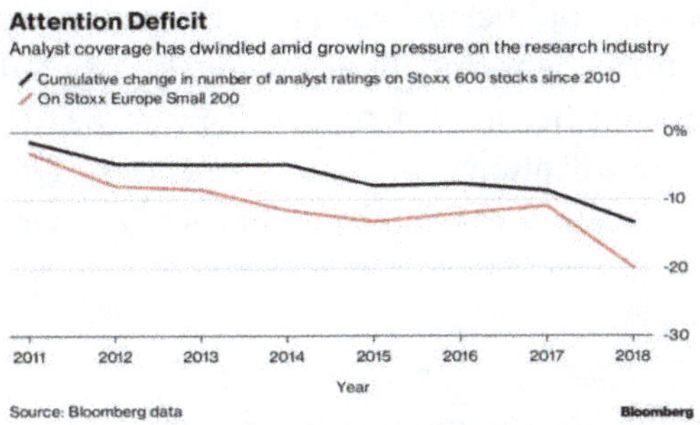

FIGURE 5 MiFID II effect on small cap analyst coverage
LEE, 2019

It would be hard to believe that a highly emotional decision would be affected by a 3-page KID at the point of sale, let alone an entire prospectus of each prospecting product. It would be much simpler to imagine that prior experience and professional advice play a much larger role in the decision-making process. As such, disclosure in and of itself is viewed as a rather soft form of protection akin to nutrition labeling laws.

Mandated discloses such as the PRIIPS KID framework portray a clear effort to empower consumers of financial services to be more self-reliant. However, the reality is that they cannot meaningfully capture the growing complexity of capital markets and financial instruments coupled with changing landscape of disclosure requirements concerning conduct of business, product oversight, governance or distribution; all of which led towards the inevitable information overload problem. The irony is that PRIIP's might just be another example of how regulators in their attempt to improve disclosure have unintendedly further complicated it.

While the discussions highlighted in this chapter did not result in definitive conclusions, it did show how these issues are constantly being reexamined after every crisis; it appears that in the aftermath of each crisis, the spotlight points at supervisory failures and cries for change are revoiced (Masciandaro & Quintyn, 2013, p. 265). Why is this the case? This can be answered from two different perspectives, which essentially reinforce each other. Firstly, in a financial system that is liberalized, any search for effectiveness at the supervisory level is met with the existing tension between the need to regulate financial systems and the objective of the latter to function freely (Masciandaro & Quintyn, 2013, p. 265). This tension faced by regulators is perfectly highlighted by the argument posed by Goodhart and Schoenmaker (1995) that "if financial institutions are free, failing is part of this freedom, but supervisors will always be blamed for it. This mismatch of intentions leads to the well-known and recurring situation where the public and politicians will blame the regulatory authority for the crises that do occur, while taking the regulators for granted otherwise" (p. 343). Ultimately, as in every free market, there will always be two sides to every trade, and as such there will always be winners and losers. This begs the question of just how far regulation can intervene in such a system without distorting it.

5 Interplay between Behavioral Finance and Investor Protection

Considering the findings from prior chapters concerning investor behavior and caveats in existing frameworks place the suitability of these traditional legal methods of investor protection in a precarious position. Nonetheless, it is pertinent to first closely examine the core complication into the normative applications of behavioral finance, before evaluating any specific implications for legislation. A crucial note that must be mentioned is that contrary to neo-classical finance and NIE, the scientific field of behavioral economic does not and never meant to impose any normative rules (Spindler, 2011, p. 325). As such, for the time being any regulatory recommendation stemming from behavioral finance must still adhere to traditional efficiency models of legal reasoning.

A distinctive factor of behavioral finance is its ability to verify the examinations of behavioral actions in a specific structure; hence apart from traditional statistical testing, it is the only other method to substantiate or refute any of the established classical economic theories (Spindler, 2011, p. 325). However, it is arguable if behavioral finance findings can be generalized—a factor by which legislators deem to be a pertinent prerequisite (Posner, 1998, p. 1552); this means that only certain framework conditions (such as variability in demographics of inspected individuals) may be categorized as the result of behavioral experiments (Arlen, 1998, p. 1766). Therefore, criticism towards behavioral finance is expected as often studies have "cherry-picked" specific anomalies, while refraining from establishing a widespread theoretical and normative structure (Fama, 1998, p. 288). However, since it has not yet been factually established that behavioral factors may result in a systemic market failure (Spindler, 2011, p. 327), further investigation into the interplay between behavioral finance and regulations may paint a clearer picture.

It is also important to establish that being aware of one's own irrational behavior does not constitute that one can also skillfully overcome irrational behavior or that regulators short of complete paternalistic control could offer methods to amend disruptive market practices caused by irrational behavior (De Meza et al., 2008, p. 3; Arlen, 1998, p. 1768). Since the purpose of behavioral finance was never meant to legally alter the traditional normative efficiency method, lawmakers mostly uphold some version of rational behavior while deliberating over normative matters (Spindler, 2011, p. 326). Lawmakers' conviction in the normative efficiency criteria stems from their belief that while legislation should be founded on reality, contract parity between transacting parties is the primary motivation in normative philosophy (Spindler, 2011, p. 327; de Meza et al., 2008, p. 62).

Must we stick to this traditional efficiency model even though we are slowly becoming more aware of our irrational tendencies? Based on the harm caused by recurring financial crisis, the answer is a definite no. Even with behavioral finance's lack of normative principles, it is crucial to at least alter established normative methods in order to mitigate some of the more destructive behavioral "distortions" (Posner, 2007, p. 23). While at first it might appear radical, behavioral finance has the potential to elevate our aged normative principles (Spindler, 2011, p. 327).

5.1 *Viability of Stricter Regulatory Frameworks*

With all these market distortions, legislators are endlessly assessing ways to improve investor protection. A totally unregulated free market solution has clearly been shown to fail; reputation mechanism, long-term learning effect, or signaling mechanisms cannot be relied upon due to the associated systemic risks that would cause them to collapse during short-term market turmoil (Spence, 1976, p. 591; Stiglitz, 1975, p. 293). Regardless even if these mechanisms were enhanced in years to come, the core issues regarding illogical behavior still exist as enhanced signaling only increases the ease of endorsing a complex investment decision, however it cannot hope to abolish the effects of irrational behavior (Spindler, 2011, p. 327). The endowment effect, herding and overconfidence will continue to exist; hence, if rational behavior assumptions based on traditional methods have proven to be insufficient, perhaps proposing a more stringent measure is the answer (Faure & Luth, 2011, p. 334).

5.1.1 Paternalism

Is it in the best interest of lawmakers and the public to replace self-correcting market mechanisms in favor of a state-sponsored "paternalistic" control over our financial decisions? Such a system would have total authority and command over all current and newly proposed financial solutions; as such, the aim would be to once and for all put an end to all asymmetry problems (Sunstein &

Thaler, 2003, p. 1162). In retrospect, such a system would replace market-based signaling and reputation mechanisms in favor of a synthetic State sponsorship over all products and services (Faure & Luth 2011, p. 353). Realistically, this is not a wise decision. Putting the inevitable issues over moral hazard aside, these State agencies would be rifled by conflicts of interests and constrained by the work overload of an inadequately skilled workforce (Faure & Luth 2011, p. 352; Springer, 2011, p. 327). In addition, it is not a given that a regulator would have more knowledge of the efficient equilibrium than a "distorted", though self-correcting market (Bainbridge, 1999, p. 1056). Hence it is highly probable that a market that is completely controlled might just swap new inefficiencies with existing ones; indirectly, such a bureaucratic system would inevitably stifle financial innovation with their unending reviews and deliberations (Spindler, 2011, p. 328).

Moreover, such a paternalistic regime would have no effect on the irrational behavior of market participants (Faure & Luth 2011, p. 353). While such a system would take tighter measures over secondary markets, it might be difficult to manage the risks associated with the unavoidable herding effects that would fallow (Spindler, 2011, p. 328). Legislation alone cannot hope to stop individuals from making bad decisions—especially if the quality signaling mechanisms are controlled by only one entity (Spindler, 2011, p. 328). In a nutshell, continued skepticism exists about the viability of managing irrational behavior even with the strictest and most radical of measures.

5.1.2 Reform Incentive Systems

As it pertains to financial intermediaries, it is crucial to equalize the risks associated with conflicts of interest and their herding behavior (Carmel et al., 2015, p. 1). While avoiding all irrational behavior through regulations may be challenging, amending the current inducement practices could indirectly counterbalance some principal agent asymmetries. As such a stricter method would pose an outright ban on all inducement practices—compelling banks to switch over to a consultation "fee" based model—in doing so, it would mitigate any conflicts typically associated with the product distribution process (Spindler, 2011, p. 329). In addition, a Chinese wall should be considered as is currently in practice with insider trading laws; as such, banks would be mandated to establish barriers between their product solutions lines and advisory service (Spindler, 2011, p. 329). Finally, rather than simply complying with disclosing conflict of interests, internal practices should progress towards stricter avoidance of any potential conflict of interest (Carmel et al., 2015, p. 2). With all due respect to MiFID II, providing financial intermediaries a loophole through discloses rather than averting their conflict of interest is "led ad absurdum" (Spindler, 2011, p. 330).

5.1.3 Enhance KYC

Current EU "Know Your Client" (KYC) laws mandate banks and certified financial advisers to gauge their prospecting clients with questions about their financial knowledge (Colaert, 2017, p. 13). In theory, every investment consultation should begin with extensively examining the client's financial experience, risk tolerance and time horizon; unfortunately in practice, this requirement is not fully complied with (Oehler et al., 2010, p. 11). It would be particularly interesting to ask a few financial advisors how their client's risk tolerance statements stood up during the 2020 market crash and the remarkably quick recovery that followed; were investment mistakes made due to some of the previously mentioned behavioral biases that were surly present during this time? Particularly, did loss aversion bias trump their perceived risk tolerance? And in parallel, is over-confidence bias doing the same during the FED induced rally following the crash?

It is doubtful if these currently overconfident retail investors would blame themselves as ill-informed in the next crash. As such, perhaps current KYC practices could be enhanced through some sort of psychometric standardized test that would more deeply gauge clients financial experience in addition to their psychological capacity; such a test would give advisors better insight into their client's true knowledge and apparent biases (Spindler, 2011, p. 330; Willis, 2009, p. 415). The documentation of such a detailed KYC test would stop the popular practice of banks claiming their clients did not reveal their risk tolerance; as such, these tests would serve a stronger foundation towards an improved consultation experience (Willis, 2009, p. 415). Additionally, these tools would further mitigate malicious exploitation of client's irrational behavior by financial intermediaries; the Lehmann Brother's certificate selling distinctly exposed how financial intermediaries could take advantage of the ignorance of investors as to the true risks associated with these certificates (Swedberg, 2010, p. 92).

A new concept that has recently gained attention is that of "open finance"; in this concept, client information is gathered and shared across financial institutions, potentially using blockchain technology which would protect client information through an encrypted decentralization solution (Moyano, & Ross, 2017, p. 412). Today, if a potential customer is shopping around, the current process is structured in such a way that a new client profile must be made by each financial institution or intermediary which provides an offer; the prospecting client must go through a new KYC questionnaire process at every prospecting institution. Setting aside the inconvenience of such a repetitive procedure, at the end your bank can only know what you have with them but are blind to your exposure with other institutions. In in order to streamline this process and enhance the quality of advice, the industry should evolve towards an "open finance" model with portable client profiles that are stored decentralized and with interconnectivity between institutions.

This information-sharing approach would enhance client experience as it can accelerate the onboarding process; in addition, it would provide valuable information to advisors who may use it to better consult their client needs and have insight into their prior financial behaviors (Moyano, & Ross, 2017, p. 422). The onboarding process of such a model would probably have big cost offsetting implication for the industry if a client profile doesn't need to be repeated at each institution. The streamlined structure of an open finance model could also mitigate a structural issue in the distribution model of European banks, specifically the issue revolving around conflicts of interest resulting from bank-owned assurance funds creating captive customers. Captive customers refer to when bank assurance groups sell their own insurance investment products to their retail bank's customers, hence the term captive customer. It means they tell you how much you're going to pay and what you're going to get, rather than asking their customers what they want and give options from their competitors. While the European commission officially likes the concept of an open finance platform, it is very unlikely to be implemented as banks have minimal economic incentives to provide their clients with an open architecture platform where it would be easy to switch to assurance providers of other financial institutions.

5.1.4 Controlled Minimum Standard

To mitigate information overload, complexity and facilitate comparability in financial product disclosures a standardized information document such as the PRIIP KID must be further enhanced (Faure & Luth, 2011, p. 352; Oehler & Wendt, 2017, p. 189). This means that every financial product that is designed for retail customers must adhere to matching informational categories and methodologies of estimated risks, liquidity, Net returns, costs (Oehler & Wendt, 2017, p. 189). The information must be presented clearly and concisely to avoid potential misunderstandings, confusion, or misinterpretation; hence it is pertinent that these documents include information that is easily understood, such as presenting information in nominal terms rather than in percentages (Faure & Luth, 2011, p. 352). To establish industry-wide best practices, regulators must offer a standardized sample that would help expedite the implementation of these enhancements (Oehler & Wendt, 2017, p. 189).

At first, this might seem like an appeal for extra regulation, but it juxtaposes this position as it allows for the removal and the coupling of various overlapping regulatory frameworks covering: insurance-linked products, mutual funds, state-subsidized private pension and packaged investment products (Oehler & Wendt, 2017, p. 189). To supervise this implementation, the disclosure documents must undergo a preapproval and periodical post-issuance inspection by the respective national competent authorities and be reviewed by consumer advocacy groups (Oehler & Wendt, 2017, p. 187).

5.2 *Beyond Disclosures*

5.2.1 Financial Literacy

Financial literacy can be defined as "the knowledge, ability, skills and confidence to make good financial decisions" (Huston, 2010, p. 296). The idea of implementing financial literacy initiatives in all stages of the educational system could be seen as the key to solve nearly all the issues revolving around comprehension and information overload. Disclosure of information assumes that the beneficiary (the reader) has sufficient knowledge and experience to understand and process it. However, what if the beneficiaries of these disclosures have a very low level of financial literacy? Even a perfect disclosure could not help if people don't understand simple concepts such as inflation, risk diversification or not to mention compound interest. The investment industry is routinely accused of pushing away any blame by excusing client misbehavior as a lack of financial literacy, but in all honestly, you cannot in a three-page PRIIP KID help if a client doesn't understand how percentages work.

The common stance in favor of government-sponsored financial literacy initiatives reflects today's social activists and policymaker's perception that financial literacy can be used as a mitigating tool in protecting investors from costly and irrational financial behaviors (Carmel, Leiser, & Spivak, 2020, p. 88). These claims however are controversial as they are supported and refuted by numerous studies; in support, Clark, Morrill, and Allen (2012) found that employees who undergo a pension seminar at their workplace chose pension planes more wisely than those who have not (p. 851). Hilgert, Hogarth, and Beverly (2003) asserted that financial literacy has significant explanatory power in informed financial decision making (p. 309), while Van Rooij et al. (2011) analysis revealed that successful equities investments are significantly correlated with financial literacy (p. 449).

While a strong correlation exists, the causal relationship between financial literacy and sound financial capability is somewhat vague; Fernandes, Lynch, and Netemeyer (2014) study assert that the two possess a non-causal relationship and that the effects of financial education only play a minimal and rapidly decaying part in financial capabilities (p. 1861). Choi et al. (2002) study found that only 15% of the people who complete investment seminars aimed at improving investment decisions actually implement the strategies learned (p. 102). Cole and Shastry (2009) findings show that financial education programs at schools did not influence student's participation in the financial markets (p. 30), while Willis's (2011) study claims that finical education courses in high school were ineffective on the basis of effectively preparing students in making financial decisions (p. 813). Willis (2011) concludes his paper with a critical note asserting that legislator's focus on financial literacy is a poor distraction from their failed regulatory effectiveness (p. 831).

The central views posed in favor of providing financial education are also being challenged from a behavioral finance stance. The minimal impact financial literacy has on financial capability could be argued under the findings of Daniel Kahneman (2011), who states that rational reasoning is hindered by its associated mental effort (p. 16). Kahneman coins this cognitive process of rational reasoning "system 2" thinking, which is attained slowly and demands great cognitive resources to produce a thoughtful perception (p. 17). As such, due to the associated high energy costs of "system 2" thinking most people rely on their intuition or "system 1" thinking in their financial decisions, which involve "rules of thumb" reasoning based upon heuristic, biases and past experiences (p. 10).

It is without a doubt that knowledge should always be viewed as a virtue, however, the uncomfortable truth is that for most of us, financial decisions are rarely based on our fundamental understanding of discounted cashflows, relative valuations or the current yield curve; in most cases, it is our short term "system 1" thinking driven by our biases and emotional reasoning (De Meza et al., 2008, p. 57; Fernandes et al., 2014, p. 33). It would seem the main problem is that the accusation of new knowledge does not necessarily translate towards a change in behavior; knowledge about what to do in a given situation and actually doing it seem to be two very different mental exercises.

The debate around the effective gain of financial literacy is unlikely to be settled soon, the aim in the meantime is to provide further insight and advocate towards a possible middle ground. According to Drexler et al. (2014) enhancing financial literacy through education only yields minimal effects, however specific educational initiates which focus on teaching basic financial aspects through useful "rules of thumb" have shown to be more effective in enhancing financial decisions (p. 3). The premise of Drexler et al. (2014) argument is the financial education faces an uphill challenge; financial knowledge requires specialized understanding in one area of life, an area that is constantly evolving with new finical services, products and distribution channels. For those who are not financial professionals, this task would inevitably demand constant attention and learning to balance the short half-life of their newly acquired knowledge (p. 2). As such, Drexler et al. 2014 argues that instead of bombarding students with short half-life information, educators should focus on providing baseline "rules of thumb" financial concepts and guidance on whom to contact when in need of financial expertise (p. 21).

5.2.2 Nudging

As discussed above, attaining financial knowledge or even admitting to ourselves of our cognitive limitations and irrational biases won't necessarily prevent us from making costly mistakes. The path towards better investor protection could perhaps be found by exploiting our behavioral inclinations to our benefit. The idea calls for information to be presented and written in such a way that it would induce investors to make choices that lawmakers deemed most suitable; this nudging technic frames information with the emphases of persuasion rather than the distribution of all information (Sunstein, 2014, p. 583).

This method speaks to the bounded rationality constraint and cognitive errors of individuals as it pertains to their assimilating of information; prospective nudges utilize the impact of the presentation of information, for example, graphic warnings on cigarette boxes are a nudge emphasizing the risks of smoking (Thaler & Sunstein 2008, p. 6). Moreover, nudging has the added benefit of accelerating an individual's decision process by giving them an initial push towards a particular direction (Madrian & Shea, 2001, p. 1149). For some time now the European Commission has been talking about creating an investment culture to fight the issue of too much money seating in bank accounts exposed to losses of purchasing power due to inflation. Breaching this lack of inertia is particularly useful for individuals who have not yet decided what they want; a presentation of options that are framed as the optimal or default choice could help nude the undecided towards a recommended choice (Madrian & Shea, 2001, p. 1185).

However, there is evidence that implies nudging may have contrary or ambiguous effects (Steinhart et al. 2013, p. 1842; Drescher et al. 2014, p. 217). Within the preview of academic and political deliberation, convincing answers to hard questions about nudges are scarce (Oehler & Wendt, 2017, p. 183); such as: on whose shoulders lies the burden of decision-making as to which choice is best suited or better yet suitable for each individual investor? What methodology is used to decide which choice is best? Does a difference exist in the manner in which clients respond to state-induced nudges vs intermediary induced nudges? Do people of different demographics react differently to nudges? (Oehler & Wendt, 2017, p. 184). Once again, such as with most regulatory deliberation a conclusive and bilateral determination on the matter is unlikely to be solved in the near future.

5.2.3 Collective Bargaining Power

The concept of a consumer advocate group allows for a non-governmental organization (NGO) to represent consumers best interest; such NGOs act as proxy "intermediaries" for consumers with the benefit of having a more nuanced view on individuals' particular needs and concerns (Oehler & Wendt, 2017, p. 189). The benefits of sturdy consumer NGO s are that investors would no longer have to solely depend on their own assessment or seek out costly advice, as these bodies would have in-depth reviews and recommendations of various available products and services (Oehler & Wendt, 2017, p. 189). As such, when faced with a complex financial choice or concern, having these organizations at one's disposal provides a secondary and more micro investor protection solution (Oehler & Wendt, 2017, p. 189).

Germany for example houses several consumer advocate NGOs (Stiftung Warentest, and Verbraucherzentralen for example). However, there is lingering doubt about their ability to perform their task in financial-specific matters; Verbraucherzentralen employs less than 100 financial professionals that in practice seek to represent approximately 83 million German residents (Oehler & Wendt, 2017, p. 189). Consumer NGOs such as these must contain legal and economic fortitude in order to fulfill their task and secure their trustworthiness; this means that they must be financially well endowed and be able to enter into class-action suits when in need of protecting consumer rights (Oehler & Wendt, 2017, p. 189). The latter reflects the fact that individual consumers usually do not file complaint proceedings as they are at cost disadvantage vis-à-vis their counterparty litigation means (Oehler & Wendt, 2017, p. 189).

5.3 *Recommendation by the High-Level Forum on the CMU*

In its aim at finalizing the implementation of a capital markets union (CMU), the European Commission launched a High-Level Forum (HLF) comprised of 28 highly qualified industry executives and academics to advise on specific policy actions for forthcoming CMU implantation (HLF, 2020, p. 2). "On 10 June 2020 the High-Level Forum published its final report—the report sets out 17 interconnected recommendations aimed at removing the biggest barriers in the EU's capital markets" (HLF, 2020, p. 2). This subchapter shall highlight five topic relevant insights and policy recommendations issued by the forum's subcommittee on Retail Investor Participation In The Area Of Distribution, Advice, Disclosure. The aim is to substantiate the chapter themes and arguments as observed by the member of the HLF.

5.3.1 Literacy

The subcommittee recognized the Member States' budgetary and political concerns over their population pension deficiency schemes. In addition to the historical lack of risk appetite in EU investment culture, individuals' lack of trust and understanding of financial markets often leads to participation hesitancy (HLF, 2020, p. 18). "Some individuals lack experience and understanding of even basic financial concepts while others are dissuaded by a lack of clear and understandable information investment—or lack of adequate and fair advice" (HLF, 2020, p. 18). As such and to no surprise, the committee emphasized the importance of establishing financial literacy programs; specifically recommending Member States implementation of EU framework on financial competence (budget panning, borrowing, investing) in their educational curriculums (HLF, 2020, p. 19). These programs should encourage the merits of retainment saving and provide guidance on responsible investing. Due to scalability, endorsement "should be given to financial literacy projects under Erasmus+" (HLF, 2020, p. 19).

5.3.2 Nudging

While the benefits of financial literacy programs would require a long time to evaluate, in the interim in order to stimulate sustainable pension coverage across all Member States an auto-enrolment function should be introduced within existing schemes; the CMU should issue a "best practices" occupational pension scheme blueprint for Member states to make use of. (HLF, 2020, p. 19). The HLF also recommends the development of an "automated advice solutions that would allow quality advice to be available for small portfolios, would avoid or mitigate conflicts of interest and potentially provide for economies of scale in the distribution of transparent investment products" (HLF, 2020, p. 21).

5.3.3 Inducements

With regards to the cause of low retail participation in capital markets, some HLF members point the finger at the potential negative effects of inducements in advisory services; they argue that the lack of objectivity could impair the consultation quality and product suitability (HLF, 2020, p. 20). Against this context, those members who voiced concerns over conflicts of interest have recommended a ban on all inducements; unsurprisingly, members currently benefiting from inducements were strongly opposed to any such ban, voicing their fears over "potential unintended consequences, including, for example, the risk of an 'advice gap' or a bias towards in-house products" (HLF, 2020, p. 20). Without a unanimous voice on the matter, the committee proposes that the CMU further examine the effects of inducements on the quality of advice; moreover, in the effort to improve investors trust in advisors the CMU is to set "harmonized rules on inducements with better transparency with comparable rules for all such products" (HLF, 2020, p. 20).

5.3.4 Disclosures

Naturally, with regards to information requirements set by various mandated disclosure frameworks (MiFID II, IDD, PRIIPS), the brunt of the criticism stemmed from members within the industry. Specifically, they voiced that for retail clients the documents are "too long, too complex, difficult to understand, not comparable and misleading" (HLF, 2020, p. 20). Moreover, with regard to presentation, they pointed out cost indicator inconsistencies between MiFID II, IDD and PRIIPS regulations (HLF, 2020, p. 103). The committee goes on to give evidence as to the ineffective engagement investors make with these documents and its lack of utility in their decision making; given the aforementioned claims that disclosure requirements are not consistent nor suitable, it is the committee recommendation that current disclosure rules be reassessed "with a view to making them more coherent, understandable and accessible in a digitally-friendly way" (HLF, 2020, p. 20).

5.3.5 Open Finance

Improving upon the current infrastructure of cross-institution data-sharing, the open finance/KYC utility initiative could "be extended to information sharing of other financial products, such as savings accounts, investment accounts, pension savings, mortgages, consumer credit and insurance products" (HLF, 2020, p. 21). Potential advisors would have access to a comprehensive overview of their client's financial history and current situation. As such, the HLF recommendation is for the CMU to "introduce a harmonized open finance regulatory framework covering financial and non-financial information relevant to facilitating financial planning or encouraging investment" (HLF, 2020, p. 21).

5.4 *Outlook*

The analysis has demonstrated how traditional assumptions of rational behavior in investor protection norms have place immense reliance on market mechanisms and investors' ability to comprehend and utilize information. Nonetheless, if conferring to findings from behavioral finance, lawmakers will need to extensively reexamine these traditional assumptions; therefore, it is of utmost importance that we redefine, refine or revise our core legal frameworks with developing insights stemming from the behavioral sciences.

Still, the time to denounce market-orientated frameworks or implement a sweeping paradigm shift emphasizing State-controlled paternalistic methods is not recommended; particularly, the still missing uniform theory of behavioral finance and its lack of normative principles further obscures an already complex legislative task. Hence, it would be more suitable to take a more gradual approach targeted at mitigating specific behavioral errors rather than enforcing a complete overhaul to existing frameworks. In addition, this study hopes to emphasize how pertinent further investigation into the long-run effects of financial education and other consumer-centric measures may better serve to engage retail investors and enhance the stability and competitiveness of the EU's Capital Markets Union.

6 Conclusion

The following chapter shall summarize the main themes by reiterating the research problem and consciously responding to the main research questions. In addition, implications for practice will be discussed followed by a few final thoughts and conclude with the possible avenues for further research on the topic.

The research problem stated that unless regulators find a sustainable and effective structural balance in their mounting regulatory frameworks, the regulatory pendulum will surely continue swinging to the determent of the industry, retail investors and to the robustness of free markets. To explore this phenomenon three primary lines of inquiries were made: RQ1: This study sought to critically examine the prevailing regulator tool of mandated discourses in the context of investor protection and its "effective gains" on information coherency and financial discipline for retail clients; it did so by critically analyzing segments from EU's investor protection frameworks (MiFID II & PRIIPS KID). Specifically, it sought to interpret the utility these frameworks have for retail investors. RQ2: In addition, this study examined the political/legal motivations and rationale behind EU disclosure regulation. RQ3: Finally, the study explored the feasibility of alternative forms of investor protection.

6.1 *Response to RQ1*

The findings suggest that while the importance of transparency is undeniable, the regulatory tool of mandated disclosures offers a rather weak form of investor protection. The findings do not dismiss disclosures entirely, rather they show that short of other accompanying measures they offer minimal utility in their desired objective of "informing" the decision process of retail investors. While transparency provides competitive pressure on costs, the utility of disclosing costs and other figures is somewhat overcome by a multitude of interdisciplinary challenges stemming from the behavioral, legal and political spheres. These challenges ultimately undermine the intended utility of disclosures, signifying skepticism regarding the need for further amendments or costly additions to current disclosure frameworks.

6.2 *Response to RQ2*

Findings suggest that the public demand for action deluge lawmakers. Many of these demands are inspired by "trouble stories"; these independent, though widely publicized events illustrate the apparent short-termism mindset rampant in the political spheres. Political pressure, public indignation, and a "sense of duty" incentivize legislators to take on a regulatory "sprinkler system" of actions as the fear of not doing enough outweighs their rationale of doing what is appropriate. As such, the findings suggest that the regulatory affinity and rationale for disclosure appear to stem from its quick implementation, low expense and broadly scoped dimension.

6.3 *Response to RQ3*

Findings further suggest that while the generationally long-term potential of financial education appears promising, as of yet, it remains unclear how regulators may use findings from behavioral finance to reform or enhance investor protection laws. While some other short-term alternative solutions were discovered, their feasibility to be harmonized across the EU is somewhat questionable. Furthermore, it would seem that neither expanding upon disclosure obligations nor enforcing a stronger paternalistic approach may suffice in this front.

6.4 *Implications for Practice*

This study has contributed significant insight into a vaguely understood field of knowledge. The "information paradigm" phenomenon was uniquely examined through the interdisciplinary lens of behavioral finance and economic analysis of law. The findings imply that there remains an urgency to find a stable, efficient and long-lasting regulatory framework that seeks to enhance investor protection while addressing the inherent limitations of mandated disclosure on market discipline.

Based on the critical analysis of the literature progress towards a holistic understanding of the phenomenon was made. Involving the discipline of behavioral finance did not only provide a unique foundational perspective on a rather legal subject matter but also stimulated some critical interdisciplinary thinking in its nexus to financial regulation. The findings of this study provide insightful and nuanced perspectives with implications touching at the heart of the European Commission and CMU desired objectives.

6.5 *Final Thoughts*

The ideals of transparency have long been rooted in the foundational blocks of EU investor protection laws, with the assumption that providing information would enable investors to make rational and informed financial decisions.

These regulatory frameworks have been finely polished in recent years, though with the support of analyzing past research this paper is lead to suggest that further frameworks or add-ons to EU's already bloated disclosure regime will be met with diminishing returns.

Essentially, the issue is that the EU never got disclosure right in the first place. We got lurched from one disclosure regime to another. Probably the best thing would be to completely rip it all up and start from scratch. Realistically, though the industry will never go for it as they have a strong status-quo mantra in which any change is negatively viewed due to the implication of millions in additional costs regardless of if it would be better their consumers. It's more important to understand that the framework should be consistent and reliable. Inside the framework, we might adjust, but do not change the framework as all market participants are working within that framework and any further pendulum swings in regimes will only further burden all parties involved.

Irrational financial decisions stemming from inherent behavioral biases and heuristics do not appear to have been mitigated by further regulatory measures to standardize and simplify information. Amongst the primary evidence of disclosures failure rests in the fact that retail investors often do not read disclosures, do not get it when they read it, and do not improve their decisions even if they can comprehend it (Ben-Shahar & Schneider 2010, p. 672). It would appear that the sacred principle of "caveat emptor" may have found itself at an impasse; the inherent regulatory disadvantage that disclosure harbors is in its flawed assumption that those who view the produced information can appropriately process it in a way that would lead them to make wiser financial decisions (Florini, 2007, p. 4).

It appears that emotional and behavioral factors such as herd mentality or overconfidence play a much larger role in investor decisions (Kammel, 2005, p. 21; Colaert, 2017, p. 10). These caveats ultimately undermine the intended utility of these financial disclosures and bring about skepticism regarding the need for any further regulatory intervention in this regard. Whilst this paper did not delve deeper into other aspects of investor protection, i.e., the conduct of business or product-related regulations, it did hope to reveal the inherent limitation of the much-beloved disclosures as a cure-all solution.

The exploratory purpose of the study aimed to shed new light on a lightly understood phenomenon in the hopes that the findings may stimulate and serve as a stepping ground for potential future research. Hence, for the number of finings covered in this paper it would be of great practical relevance to further investigate them in a quantitative fashion, for instance:

- Assessing the impact of research unbundling on SME competitiveness.
- Analyzing the sociological characteristics of all active EU retail investors.
- Assessing inducements effect on the quality and biasness of advice.

- Analyzing the dominant distribution channels by each EU jurisdiction.
- Measuring the gap between purchased financial instruments that were advised upon and those which were sold on an execution-only basis.
- Measuring the relationship between the cost of advice and the propensity for retail clients to seek advice.
- Additionally, these past few years demonstrated the relevancy of examining the social aspect of financial behavior; the recent surge of retail investors entering the markets and collaborating through social media has potentially led to some massive volatility in small to medium cap stocks. Qualitatively examining such a phenomenon would undoubtedly prove relevant to both the behavioralist and financial regulators.

As a final remark, this paper must reiterate that whilst it was heavily critical of disclosure, it does not outright dismiss it as redundant. It does not suggest that providing transparency to where there is none is unbeneficial, but rather that by itself it stands lacking in carrying out its intended use as a tool for investor protection. While there is some validity to arguments of enhancing transparency, they fall short in proving that in doing so they will provide sufficient protection under the weight of inherent uncertainties and irrationalities in financial markets.

Abbreviations

CMU	Capital Markets Union
CRA	Credit Rating Agency
EFAMA	European Fund and Asset Management Association
EIOPA	European Insurance and Occupational Pensions Authority
EMH	Efficient Market Hypothesis
ESA	European Supervisory Authority
ESFS	European System of Financial Supervision
ESMA	European Securities and Markets Authority
ESRB	European Systemic Risk Board
EU	European Union
FSMA	Financial Services and Markets Authority
GDP	Gross domestic product
GFC	Great Financial Crisis
HLF	High-Level Forum
IDD	Insurance Distribution Directive
IHP	Intermediate Holding Period

IPA	Interpretative phenomenological analysis
IPISC	Investor Protection and Intermediaries Standing Committee
KID	Key Information Document
KYC	Know Your Client
MiFID	Markets in Financial Instruments Directive
MiFIR	Markets in Financial Instruments Regulation
MRI	Magnetic resonance imaging
NCA	National Competent Authority
NGO	Non-Governmental Organization
NIE	New Institutional Economics
OCF	Ongoing Cost Figures
PRIIP	Packaged Retail Investment and Insurance-Based Products
RHP	Recommended holding period
RiY	Reduction-in-Yield
S&P	Standard and Poors
SCI	Summary Cost Indicator
SME	Small-to-Medium Enterprise
TCO	Total Cost of Ownership
UCITS	Undertakings for Collective Investments in Transferable Securities

Notes on Contributor

Daniel Bar Aharon, MA (2021), Lauder Business School, Vienna, Austria. Daniel is a dual citizen of Israel and the US. He currently serves as a financial analyst at a multinational corporation. This is his first publication.

References

Ananny, M., & Crawford, K. (2018). Seeing without knowing: Limitations of the transparency ideal and its application to algorithmic accountability. *New Media & Society*, *20*(3), 973–989. http://dx.doi.org/10.1177/1461444816676645.

Andreassen, P. B. (1987). On the social psychology of the stock market: Aggregate attributional effects and the repressiveness of prediction. *Journal of Personality and Social Psychology*, *53*(3), 490. http://dx.doi.org/10.1037/0022-3514.53.3.490.

Andreassen, P. B. (1990). Judgmental extrapolation and market overreaction: On the use and disuse of news. *Journal of Behavioral Decision Making*, *3*(3), 153–174. http://dx.doi.org/10.1002/bdm.3960030302.

Appelbaum, B. (2013, October 14). Economists clash on theory, but will still share the Nobel. *The New York Times*. Retrieved February 20, 2021, from https://www.nytimes.com/2013/10/15/business/3-american-professors-awarded-nobel-in-economic-sciences.html.

Arlen, J. (1998). The future of behavioral economic analysis of law. *Vanderbilt Law Review*, *51*, 1765–1788.

Bainbridge, S. M. (1999). Mandatory disclosure: A behavioral analysis. *University of Cincinnati Law Review*, *68*, 1023. http://dx.doi.org/10.2139/ssrn.329880.

Barber, B. M., & Odean, T. (2001). Boys will be boys: Gender, overconfidence, and common stock investment. *The Quarterly Journal of Economics*, *116*(1), 261–292. http://dx.doi.org/10.1162/003355301556400.

Barber, B. M., & Odean, T. (2013). The behavior of individual investors. In *Handbook of the Economics of Finance*, 2, 1533–1570. http://dx.doi.org/10.1016/B978-0-44-459406-8.00022-6.

Bar-Gill, O. (2008). The law, economics and psychology of subprime mortgage contracts. *Cornell Law Review*, *94*, 1073.

Baron, J. (2000). *Thinking and deciding* (3rd ed.). Cambridge, United Kingdom: Cambridge University Press.

Barro, R. J. (2006). Rare disasters and asset markets in the twentieth century. *The Quarterly Journal of Economics*, *121*(3), 823–866. http://dx.doi.org/10.1162/qjec.121.3.823.

Ben-Shahar, O., & Schneider, C. (2010). The failure of mandated disclosure. *University of Chicago Law & Economics, Paper No. 516* and *University of Michigan Law & Economics, Empirical Legal Studies Center, Paper No. 10-008*. http://dx.doi.org/10.2139/ssrn.1567284.

Bernstein, W. J., & Ryan, C. (2002). *The Four Pillars of Investing: lessons for building a winning portfolio*. New York, New York: McGraw-Hill.

Blankespoor, E., Dehaan, E., Wertz, J., & Zhu, C. (2019). Why do individual investors disregard accounting information? The roles of information awareness and acquisition costs. *Journal of Accounting Research*, *57*(1), 53–84.

Bodie, Z. (2009). *Investments*. Tata, India: McGraw-Hill Education.

Bryman, A. (2016). *Social research methods*. Oxford, United Kingdom: Oxford University Press.

Camerer, C. (1995). Individual Decision Making. In J. H. Kagel & A. E. Roth (Eds.), *The handbook of experimental economics* (pp. 587–703). Princeton, New Jersey: Princeton University Press. http://dx.doi.org/10.2307/j.ctvzsmff5.12.

Camerer, C., Issacharoff, S., Loewenstein, G., O'donoghue, T., & Rabin, M. (2003). Regulation for Conservatives: Behavioral Economics and the Case for Asymmetric Paternalism. *University of Pennsylvania Law Review*, *151*(3), 1211–1254. http://dx.doi.org/10.2307/3312889.

Camerer, C., Loewenstein, G., & Weber, M. (1989). The curse of knowledge in economic settings: An experimental analysis. *The Journal of Political Economy, 97*(5), 1232–1254. http://dx.doi.org/10.1086/261651.

Caplan, B. (2001). Rational irrationality and the micro foundations of political failure. *Public Choice, 107*(3), 311–331.

Carmel, E., Carmel, D., Leiser, D., & Spivak, A. (2015). Facing a biased adviser while choosing a retirement plan: The impact of financial literacy and fair disclosure. *Journal of Consumer Affairs, 49*(3), 576–595. http://dx.doi.org/10.1111/joca.12083.

Chicago Booth Review. (2016, June 30). *Are markets efficient?* [Video File]. YouTube. Retrieved June 12, 2021 from https://www.youtube.com/watch?v=bM9bYOBuKF4.

Choi, J. J., Laibson, D., Madrian, B. C., & Metrick, A. (2002). Defined contribution pensions: Plan rules, participant choices, and the path of least resistance. *Tax Policy and the Economy, 16*, 67–113. http://dx.doi.org/10.1086/654750.

Chopra, N., Lakonishok, J., & Ritter, J. R. (1992). Measuring abnormal performance: do stocks overreact? *Journal of Financial Economics, 31*(2), 235–268.

Clark, R. L., Morrill, M. S., & Allen, S. G. (2012). The role of financial literacy in determining retirement plans. *Economic Inquiry, 50*(4), 851–866. http://dx.doi.org/10.1111/j.1465-7295.2011.00390.x.

Colaert, V. (2017). Building blocks of investor protection: All-embracing regulation tightens its grip. *Journal of European Consumer and Market Law, 6*, 229. http://dx.doi.org/10.2139/ssrn.2943985.

Cole, S. A., & Shastry, G. K. (2009). *Smart money: The effect of education, cognitive ability, and financial literacy on financial market participation*. Boston, Massachusetts: Harvard Business School.

Cooper, M. J., Dimitrov, O., & Rau, P. R. (2001). A rose. com by any other name. *The Journal of Finance, 56*(6), 2371–2388. http://dx.doi.org/10.1111/0022-1082.00408.

Covitz, D. M., & Harrison, P. (2003). *Testing conflicts of interest at bond rating agencies with market anticipation: Evidence that reputation incentives dominate*. Board of Governors of the Federal Reserve System (US). http://dx.doi.org/10.2139/ssrn.512402.

Crockett, A., Harris, T., Mishkin, F. S., & White, E. N. (2003). *Conflicts of Interest in the Financial Services Industry: What should we do about them?* (No. 5). Center for Economic Policy Research.

Davies, H., & Green, D. (2013). *Global financial regulation: The essential guide*. Hoboken, New Jersey: John Wiley & Sons.

De Bondt, W. F., & Thaler, R. H. (1990). Do security analysts overreact? *The American Economic Review*, 52–57.

De Meza, D., Irlenbusch, B., & Reyniers, D. (2008). Financial capability: A behavioral economics perspective. *Consumer Research, 69*, 192–193.

Deaves, R., Dine, C., & Horton, W. (2006). *How are investment decisions made?* Report Commissioned by the Task Force to Modernize Securities Legislation in Canada.

Deloitte. (2016). What will be the impact of MiFID II on the investment fund distribution landscape? Retrieved June 4, 2021, from https://www2.deloitte.com/lu/en/pages/investment-management/articles/mifid2-cross-border.html.

Dhar, R. (1997). Consumer preference for a no-choice option. *Journal of Consumer Research, 24*(2), 215–231. http://dx.doi.org/10.1086/209506.

Directive 2014/65/EU. (2014). Markets in financial instruments directive. European Parliament, Council of the European Union. https://eur-lex.europa.eu/legal-content/EN/TXT/PDF/?uri=CELEX:32014L0065.

Drescher, L. S., Roosen, J., & Marette, S. (2014). The effects of traffic light labels and involvement on consumer choices for food and financial products. *International Journal of Consumer Studies, 38*, 217–227. http://dx.doi.org/10.1111/ijcs.12086.

Drexler, A., Fischer, G., & Schoar, A. (2014). Keeping it simple: Financial literacy and rules of thumb. *American Economic Journal: Applied Economics, 6*, 1–31. http://dx.doi.org/10.1257/app.6.2.1.

Du, M., Niessen-Ruenzi, A., & Odean, T. (2019). Stock repurchasing bias of mutual funds. http://dx.doi.org/10.2139/ssrn.3247066.

Easterbrook, F. H., & Fischel, D. R. (1984). Mandatory disclosure and the protection of investors. *Virginia Law Review, 70*(4), 669–715. http://dx.doi.org/10.2307/1073082.

ESMA/2014/1569. (2014). *ESMA's Technical advice to the Commission on MiFID II and MiFIR.* https://www.esma.europa.eu/sites/default/files/library/2015/11/2014-1569_final_report_-_esmas_technical_advice_to_the_commission_on_mifid_ii_and_mifir.pdf.

Etzioni, A. (2010). Is Transparency the Best Disinfectant? *Journal of Political Philosophy, 18*(4), 389–404. http://dx.doi.org/10.2139/ssrn.2731880.

Eugene, B., & Robert, K. (1982). *Going by the book: The problem of regulatory unreasonableness.* New Brunswick, New Jersey: Transaction Publishers.

Fama, E. (1970). Efficient Capital Markets: A Review of Theory and Empirical Work. *Journal of Finance, 25*(2), 383–417. http://dx.doi.org/10.2307/2325486.

Fama, E. F. (1998). Market efficiency, long-term returns, and behavioral finance. *Journal of Financial Economics, 49*(3), 283–306. http://dx.doi.org/10.2139/ssrn.15108.

Faure, M. G., & Luth, H. A. (2011). Behavioral economics in unfair contract terms. *Journal of Consumer Policy, 34*(3), 337–358. http://dx.doi.org/10.1007/s10603-011-9162-9.

Ferguson, N. (2008). *The ascent of money: A financial history of the world.* London, United Kingdom: Penguin.

Fernandes, D., Lynch, J. G., Jr., & Netemeyer, R. G. (2014). Financial literacy, financial education, and downstream financial behaviors. *Management Science, 60*(8), 1861–1883. http://dx.doi.org/10.1287/mnsc.2013.1849.

Fischoff, B. (1982). Debiasing. In Kahneman, D., Slovic, S. P., Slovic, P., & Tversky, A. (Eds.), *Judgment under uncertainty: Heuristics and biases.* Cambridge, United Kingdom: Cambridge University Press.

Flannery, M. J., & Sorescu, S. M. (1996). Evidence of bank market discipline in subordinated debenture yields: 1983–1991. *The Journal of Finance, 51*(4), 1347–1377. http://dx.doi.org/10.2307/2329397.

Florini, A. (2007). *The right to know: transparency for an open world.* New York, New York: Columbia University Press. http://dx.doi.org/10.7312/flor14158.

Frydman, C., & Camerer, C. (2016). Neural evidence of regret and its implications for investor behavior. *The Review of Financial Studies, 29*(11), 3108–3139. http://dx.doi.org/10.1093/rfs/hhw010.

Goble, E., Austin, W., Larsen, D., Kreitzer, L., & Brintnell, E. S. (2012). Habits of mind and the split-mind effect: When computer-assisted qualitative data analysis software is used in phenomenological research. *Qualitative Social Research, 13*(2), 1–22. https://doi.org/10.17169/fqs-13.2.1709.

Godwin, A., & Ramsay, I. (2015). Financial products and short-form disclosure documents: A comparative analysis of six jurisdictions. *Capital Markets Law Journal, 10*, 212–238. http://dx.doi.org/10.1093/cmlj/kmv018.

Gold, H. (2016). Consumer protection takes more than transparency. *Chicago Booth Review.* Retrieved June 3, 2021 from https://review.chicagobooth.edu/behavioral-science/2016/article/consumer-protection-takes-more-transparency.

Goodhart, C. A. (2007). Financial supervision from a historical perspective. *The Structure of Financial Regulation, 43.* http://dx.doi.org/10.4324/9780203962312.ch2.

Goodhart, C. A. E. (2008). The background to the 2007 financial crisis. *International Economics and Economic Policy, 4*(4), 331–346. http://dx.doi.org/10.1007/s10368-007-0098-0.

Graham, B. (1965). *The intelligent investor.* New York, New York: Harper & Row.

Greenspan, A. (2003). *Remarks by Alan Greenspan Chairman, Board of Governors of the Federal Reserve System via Satellite Before the Conference on Bank Structure and Competition.* Federal Reserve Bank of Chicago, Conference on Bank Structure and Competition. Retrieved January 11, 2021 from https://fraser. stlouisfed.org/title/statements-speeches-alan-greenspan-452/remarks-via-satellite-conference-bank-structure-competition-federal-reserve-bank-chicago-8790/fulltext.

Hauser, J. (1993). How consumers allocate their time when searching for information. *Journal of Marketing Research, 30*(4), 452–466. http://dx.doi.org/10.2307/3172690.

Herrmann-Pillath, C. (1994). Evolutionary rationality, homo economicus, and the foundations of social order. *Journal of Social and Evolutionary Systems, 17*(1), 41–69. http://dx.doi.org/10.1016/1061-7361(94)90006-X.

High-Level Forum on Capital Markets Union. (2020). *A New Vision for Europe's Capital Markets: Final Report of the High-Level Forum on the Capital Markets.* Retrieved May 27, 2021 from https://ec.europa.eu/info/publications/cmu-high-level-forum_en#200610.

Hilgert, M. A., Hogarth, J. M., & Beverly, S. G. (2003). Household financial management: The connection between knowledge and behavior. *Federal Reserve Bulletin, 89*, 309.

Hirshleifer, D. (2001). Investor psychology and asset pricing. *Journal of Finance, 56*(4), 1533–1597. http://dx.doi.org/10.1111/0022-1082.00379.

Hood, C. (2006). *Transparency in historical perspective*. Oxford, United Kingdom: Oxford University Press.

Hood, C., & Heald, D. (2006). *Transparency: The key to better governance?* Oxford, United Kingdom: Oxford University Press http://dx.doi.org/10.5871/bacad/9780197263839.003.0001.

Hoskins, S. M., & Labonte, M. (2015). An analysis of the regulatory burden on small banks.

Huston, S. J. (2010). Measuring financial literacy. *Journal of Consumer Affairs, 44*(2), 296–316. http://dx.doi.org/10.1111/j.1745-6606.2010.01170.x.

Islam, R. (2006). Does more transparency go along with better governance? *Economics & Politics, 18*(2), 121–167. http://dx.doi.org/10.1111/j.1468-0343.2006.00166.x.

Jacques, L. (2009). *The High-Level Group of Financial Supervision in the EU*. Retrieved May 27, 2021 from http://ec.europa. eu/internal_market/finances/docs/de_larosiere_report-en.pdf.

Jin, G. Z., Luca, M., & Martin, D. (2015). *Is no news (perceived as) bad news? An experimental investigation of information disclosure* (No. w21099). National Bureau of Economic Research. http://dx.doi.org/10.2139/ssrn.2591450.

Kahneman, D. (2003). A perspective on judgment and choice: mapping bounded rationality. *American psychologist, 58*(9), 697–720. http://dx.doi.org/10.1037/0003-066X.58.9.697.

Kahneman, D. (2011). *Thinking, fast and slow*. New York, New York: Macmillan.

Kahneman, D., Knetsch, J. L., & Thaler, R. H. (1991). Anomalies: The endowment effect, loss aversion, and status quo bias. *Journal of Economic Perspectives, 5*(1), 193–206. http://dx.doi.org/10.1257/jep.5.1.193.

Kahneman, D., & Tversky, A. (1973). On the psychology of prediction. *Psychological Review, 80*(4), 237. http://dx.doi.org/10.1037/h0034747.

Kahneman, D., & Tversky, A. (1979). Prospect theory: An analysis of decision under risk. *Econometrica, 47*(2), 263–292. http://dx.doi.org/10.2307/1914185.

Kammel, A. J. (2015). Government Versus Markets—A Change in Financial Regulation. In *The Changing Landscape of Global Financial Governance and the Role of Soft Law* (pp. 1–27). Leiden, Netherlands: Brill Nijhoff. http://dx.doi.org/10.1163/9789004280328_003.

Keynes, J. M. (1937). The general theory of employment. *The Quarterly Journal of Economics, 51*(2), 209–223. http://dx.doi.org/10.2307/1882087.

Klimesch, D., & Klar, F. (2020, February 6). Time to get ready for MiFID III? *Deltaconx*. Retrieved 4, June 2021, from https://deltaconx.com/2020/02/06/time-to-get-ready-for-mifid-iii-part-i-drawing-the-battle-lines/.

Knight, F. H. (1921). *Risk, uncertainty and profit*. Boston, Massachusetts: Houghton Mifflin.

Lai, S. M., Liu, C. L., & Wang, T. (2014). Increased disclosure and investment efficiency. *Asia-Pacific Journal of Accounting & Economics*, *21*(3), 308–327. http://dx.doi.org/10.1080/16081625.2012.741791.

Lang, M. H., Pinto, J., & Sul, E. (2019). MiFID II unbundling and sell side analyst research. http://dx.doi.org/10.2139/ssrn.3408198.

Lee, S. (2019, January 3). Research Analysts' Existential Crisis Enters MiFID II Era. *Bloomberg*. Retrieved June 4, 2021, from https://www.bloomberg.com/news/articles/2019-01-03/the-research-analyst-s-existential-crisis-enters-mifid-ii-era.

Leuz, C., & Verrecchia, R. E. (2000). The economic consequences of increased disclosure. *Journal of Accounting Research*, *38*, 91–124. http://dx.doi.org/10.2307/2672910.

Liu, P., & Thakor, A. V. (1984). Interest yields, credit ratings, and economic characteristics of state bonds: An empirical analysis. *Journal of Money, Credit and Banking*, *16*(3), 344–351.

Madrian, B. C., & Shea, D. F. (2001). The power of suggestion: Inertia in 401 (k) participation and savings behavior. *The Quarterly Journal of Economics*, *116*(4), 1149–1187. http://dx.doi.org/10.1162/003355301753265543.

Malkiel, B. G. (2003). The efficient market hypothesis and its critics. *Journal of Economic Perspectives*, *17*(1), 59–82. http://dx.doi.org/10.1257/089533003321164958.

MARKT/2014/060/G. (2015). *Consumer testing study of the possible new format and content for retail disclosures of packaged retail and insurance-based investment products final report*. Brussels, European Commission. Retrieved May 24, 2021 from https://ec.europa.eu/info/sites/default/files/consumer-testing-study-2015_en.pdf.

Masciandaro, D., & Quintyn, M. (2013). The evolution of financial supervision: the continuing search for the holy grail. SUERF-The European Money and Finance Forum.

McDonald, R. L., & Rietz, T. A. (2018). *Ratings and asset allocation: An experimental analysis* (No. w25046). National Bureau of Economic Research.

McGrath, L. (2020, March 28). Zoom Technologies Trading Suspended After Ticker Confusion. *Bloomberg*. Retrieved 19, May 2021, from https://www.bloomberg.com/news/articles/2020-03-26/zoom-technologies-trading-suspended-amid-ticker-confusion.

Micklitz, H. W. (2004). The principles of European contract law and the protection of the weaker party. *Journal of Consumer Policy*, *27*(3), 339–356. http://dx.doi.org/10.1023/B:COPO.0000040516.53187.ff.

Moloney, N. (2008). *EC securities regulation* (No. 2nd). Oxford, United Kingdom: Oxford University Press.

Moyano, J. P., & Ross, O. (2017). KYC optimization using distributed ledger technology. *Business & Information Systems Engineering*, *59*(6), 411–423.

Neal, L. (2000). A shocking view of economic history. *Journal of Economic History*, *60*(2), 317–334. http://dx.doi.org/10.1017/S0022050700025110.

Oehler, A., Höfer, A., Horn, M., & Wendt, S. (2018). Do mutual fund ratings provide valuable information for retail investors? *Studies in Economics and Finance, 35*(1), 137. http://dx.doi.org/10.1108/SEF-05-2017-0120.

Oehler, A., Höfer, A., & Wendt, S. (2014). Do key investor information documents enhance retail investors' understanding of financial products? Empirical evidence. *Journal of Financial Regulation and Compliance*, 22(2), 115–127. http://dx.doi.org/10.1108/JFRC-10-2013-0035.

Oehler, A., & Wendt, S. (2017). Good consumer information: The Information Paradigm at its (dead) end? *Journal of Consumer Policy, 40*(2), 179–191. http://dx.doi.org/10.1007/s10603-016-9337-5.

O'Neill, O. (2006). Transparency and the ethics of communication. In *Proceedings-British Academy* (Vol. 1, No. 135, pp. 75–90). Oxford, United Kingdom: Oxford University Press. http://dx.doi.org/10.5871/bacad/9780197263839.003.0005.

Pattanayak, S. (2018). *Fiscal Transparency Handbook (2018)*. International Monetary Fund. Retrieved from https://www.elibrary.imf.org/view/IMF069/24788-9781484331859/24788-9781484331859/24788-9781484331859.xml?code=fth.

Plato-Shinar, R., & Weber, R. H. (2015). Consumer Protection through Soft Law in an Era of Global Financial Crisis. In Weiss, F. & Kammel, A. (Eds.), *The Changing Landscape of Global Financial Governance and the Role of Soft Law* (pp. 233–257). Leiden, Netherlands: Brill Nijhoff.

Posner, R. (1998). Rational choice, behavioral economics and the law. *Stanford Law Review, 50*(5), 1551–1576. http://dx.doi.org/10.2307/1229305.

Posner, R. (2007). *Economic analysis of law.* (7th ed.) New York, New York: Aspen Publishers.

Prat, A. (2005). The wrong kind of transparency. *American Economic Review, 95*(3), 862–877. http://dx.doi.org/10.1257/0002828054201297.

Regulation 1286/2014/EU. (2014). Key information documents for packaged retail and insurance-based investment products (PRIIPS). European Parliament, Council of the European Union. https://eur-lex.europa.eu/legal-content/EN/ALL/?uri=CELEX%3A32014R1286.

Regulation 2017/1129/EU. (2017). The prospectus to be published when securities are offered to the public or admitted to trading on a regulated market. European Parliament, Council of the European Union. https://eur-lex.europa.eu/legal-content/EN/TXT/PDF/?uri=CELEX:32017R1129.

Ripken, S. K. (2006). The dangers and drawbacks of the disclosure antidote: Toward a more substantive approach to securities regulation. *Baylor Law Review, 58*, 139.

Robinson, G. (2017). One third UK firms 'underprepared' for MiFID II despite tough penalties warning. Retrieved June 4, 2021, from https://www.internationalinvestment.net/internationalinvestment/news/3505298/uk-firms-%E2%80%98underprepared%E2%80%99-mifid-ii-despite-tough-penalties-warning.

Saldaña, J. (2021). *The coding manual for qualitative researchers*. Thousand Oaks, California: Sage.

Salzberger, E. M. (2008). Law and Economics in the 21st Century. In: Eger, T., Bigus, J., Ott, C., von Wangenheim, G. (Eds.) *Internationalisierung des Rechts und seine ökonomische Analyse*. Wiesbaden, Germany: Gabler. https://doi.org/10.1007/978-3-8350-5582-7_2.

Samuelson, W., & Zeckhauser, R. (1988). Status quo bias in decision making. *Journal of Risk and Uncertainty*, *1*(1), 7–47. http://dx.doi.org/10.1007/BF00055564.

Scharfstein, D., & Stein, J. (1990). Herd behavior and investment. *The American Economic Review*, *80*(3), 465–479.

Schwarcz, S. L. (2008). Disclosure's Failure in the Subprime Mortgage Crisis. *Utah Law Review*, 1109.

Selten, R. (1990). Bounded rationality. *Journal of Institutional and Theoretical Economics*, *146*, 649–658.

Shefrin, H., & Statman, M. (1985). The disposition to sell winners too early and ride losers too long: Theory and evidence. *The Journal of Finance*, *40*(3), 777–790. http://dx.doi.org/10.1111/j.1540-6261.1985.tb05002.x.

Shiller, R. (2000). *Irrational exuberance*. Princeton, New Jersey: Princeton University Press.

Shiller, R. J. (1981). Do Stock Prices Move Too Much to be Justified by Subsequent Changes in Dividends? *The American Economic Review*, *71*(3), 421–436.

Shiller, R. J. (2000). Irrational exuberance. *Philosophy and Public Policy Quarterly*, *20*(1), 18–23.

Simon, H. A. (1955). A behavioral model of rational choice. *Quarterly Journal of Economics*, *69*(1),99–118. http://dx.doi.org/10.2307/1884852.

Smith, G., Venkatraman, M. P., & Dholakia, R. R. (1999). Diagnosing the search cost effect: Waiting time and the moderating impact of prior category knowledge. *Journal of Economic Psychology*, 20(3), 285–314. http://dx.doi.org/10.1016/S0167-4870(99)00010-0.

Solomon, D. H., Soltes, E., & Sosyura, D. (2014). Winners in the spotlight: Media coverage of fund holdings as a driver of flows. *Journal of Financial Economics*, *113*(1), 53–72. http://dx.doi.org/10.1016/j.jfineco.2014.02.009.

Spence, M. (1976). Symposium: The economics of information: Informational aspects of market structure: An introduction. *Quarterly Journal of Economics*, *90*(4), 591–597.

Spindler, G. (2011). Behavioral finance and investor protection regulations. *Journal of Consumer Policy*, *34*(3), 315. http://dx.doi.org/10.1007/s10603-011-9165-6.

Statman, M. (2008). What is behavioral finance? *Handbook of finance*, 2. http://dx.doi.org/10.1002/9780470404324.hof002009.

Statman, M. (2019). *Behavioral Finance: The Second Generation*. Charlottesville, Virginia: CFA Institute Research Foundation. http://dx.doi.org/10.1142/9789813279469_0001.

Steinhart, Y., Carmon, Z., & Trope, Y. (2013). Warnings of adverse side effects can backfire over time. *Psychological Science, 24*(9), 1842–1847. http://dx.doi.org/10.1177/0956797613478948.

Stiglitz, J. E. (1975). The theory of screening, education, and the distribution of income. *The American Economic Review, 65*(3), 283–300.

Strathern, M. (2000). The tyranny of transparency. *British Educational Research Journal, 26*(3), 309–321. http://dx.doi.org/10.1080/713651562.

Sunstein, C. R. (2014). Nudging: a very short guide. *Journal of Consumer Policy, 37*(4), 583–588. http://dx.doi.org/10.1007/s10603-014-9273-1.

Sunstein, C. R., & Thaler, R. H. (2003). Libertarian paternalism is not an oxymoron. *The University of Chicago Law Review, 70*(4), 1159–1202. http://dx.doi.org/10.2307/1600573.

Swedberg, R. (2010). The structure of confidence and the collapse of Lehman Brothers. In *Markets on trial: The economic sociology of the US financial crisis: Part A.* West Yorkshire, United Kingdom: Emerald Group Publishing Limited. http://dx.doi.org/10.1108/S0733-558X(2010)000030A007.

Taleb, N. (2005). *Fooled by randomness: The hidden role of chance in life and in the markets* (Vol. 1). New York, New York: Random House.

Taleb, N. (2007). *The black swan: The impact of the highly improbable* (Vol. 2). New York, New York: Random House.

Thaler, R. H. (1985). Mental accounting and consumer choice. *Marketing Science, 4*(3), 199–214. http://dx.doi.org/10.1287/mksc.4.3.199.

Thaler, R. H. (2016). Behavioral economics: Past, present, and future. *American Economic Review, 106*(7), 1577–1600. http://dx.doi.org/10.1257/aer.106.7.1577.

Thaler, R. H., & Sunstein, C. R. (2008). *Nudge: Improving Decisions About Health, Wealth, And Happiness.* London, United Kingdom: Penguin.

Thaler, R. H., Tversky, A., Kahneman, D., & Schwartz, A. (1997). The effect of myopia and loss aversion on risk taking: An experimental test. *The Quarterly Journal of Economics, 112*(2), 647–661. http://dx.doi.org/10.1162/003355397555226.

The Sveriges Riksbank Prize in Economic Sciences in Memory of Alfred Nobel (2013). Retrieved 20 February 2021, from https://www.nobelprize.org/prizes/economic-sciences/2013/press-release/.

Tversky, A., & Kahneman, D. (1974). Judgment under uncertainty: Heuristics and biases. *Science, 185*(4157), 1124–1131. http://dx.doi.org/10.1126/science.185.4157.1124.

Tversky, A., & Kahneman, D. (1986). Rational choice and the framing of decisions. *Journal of Business, 59*(4), 251–265. http://dx.doi.org/10.1086/296365.

Van der Heide, A., & Želinský, D. (2021). Level up your money game: an analysis of gamification discourse in financial services. *Journal of Cultural Economy*, 1–21. https://doi.org/10.1080/17530350.2021.1882537.

Van Rooij, M., Lusardi, A., & Alessie, R. (2011). Financial literacy and stock market participation. *Journal of Financial Economics, 101*(2), 449–472. http://dx.doi.org/10.1016/j.jfineco.2011.03.006.

Wang, S. (2021). Consumers beware: How Are Your Favorite "Free" Investment Apps Regulated? *Duke Law & Tech Review, 19*, 43.

Weiss, F., & Kammel, A. (2015). *The Changing Landscape of Global Financial Governance and the Role of Soft Law*. Leiden, Netherlands: Brill.

Willis, L. E. (2006). Decision making and the limits of disclosure: The problem of predatory lending: Price. *Maryland Law Review, 65*, 707.

World Bank Group. (2020). *Global Financial Development Report 2019/2020: Bank Regulation and Supervision a Decade After the Global Financial Crisis*. World Bank Group. Retrieved May 14, 2021 from https://www.worldbank.org/en/publication/gfdr.

Wursthorn, M., & Choi, E. (2020, August 20). Does Robinhood make it too easy to trade? From free stocks to confetti. *Wall Street Journal*. Retrieved June 17, 2021 from https://www.wsj.com/articles/confetti-free-stocks-does-robinhoods-design-make-trading-too-easy-11597915801.

www.ingramcontent.com/pod-product-compliance
Lightning Source LLC
Chambersburg PA
CBHW072244240926
51846CB00012B/598
* 9 7 8 9 0 0 4 5 3 7 0 2 6 *